MODERN CAREER MANAGEMENT

Career and job search secrets: orient yourself, stand out from the crowd, and get hired in today's market

JIM MOLLOY AND M. BRANT BUTLER

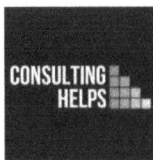

CONSULTING HELPS

Consulting HELPS
(Helping Everyone Learn Professional Skills)

www.ConsultingHELPSYou.com

Copyright

Modern Career Management

Career and job search secrets: orient yourself, stand out from the crowd, and get hired in today's market

ISBN: 978-1-7359479-0-7 (Paperback)

ISBN: 978-1-7359479-1-4 (eBook)

Library of Congress Control Number: 9781735947907

Publisher: Consulting HELPS www.ConsultingHELPSYou.com

First Edition November 2020

Acknowledgements

We would like to thank all the companies that helped us learn to keep our skills sharp in times of change. The inspiration of this book is a result of decades of career transitions, coaching others, some lessons learned on our own, and with guidance from our colleagues, friends and loved ones.

Thank you!

- **Our Wives** (for putting up with us), proofreading and making sure we don't do anything silly.
- Latayne Scott for offering her time and wisdom to help us put our best stories and advice forward.
- Russell Weaver and Amy J. P. Chang for sharing their insight from the perspective in the Talent Acquisition space.
- Kevin Fay for taking the time to be our first official "reader" of the story and help us bring our message to the next level!
- www.NJBobro.com, NJ Bobro Career Coaching and Consulting for sharing such a great graphic on the "Career Lattice"
- Carolyn Willis – Proofreader, Editor in Chief

Thank you to our Moms, and Moms everywhere who always have encouraging things to say that help us to take our next step and move forward, especially when we feel like we are moving backwards or stuck.

Table of Contents

Preface: What is Modern Career Management?

Life is a collection of memories, based on experiences. Your career is a culmination of applied skills and experiences in a professional setting. You can let fate decide your career, or you can set specific career goals to chart your progress and get where you want to be.

Career Management is Lifelong

According to a study by the US Bureau of Labor and Statistics (BLS), most workers spend five years or less in a job. What does that mean for you? You need to have a strategy and skills to help you during multiple career transitions in your lifetime. This also means that on average, men and women in the workforce will have more than 12 jobs before they retire.[1]

What are my career interests? Why should I care?

Research has shown that in our 20s, our career interests tend to stay remarkably stable. If we can find jobs compatible with our interest, work won't be a four-letter word; instead we embrace a six-letter word in its place: career. When we are working in our career and it aligns with our interests and goals, we make better contributions.

Why don't I just start on the ground level; then through promotions get into the job I want?

There are very few people who join a company at the start of their career and then retire from that same company. The corporate ladder doesn't exist like it did decades ago. Most people don't have an option to climb a "ladder" to reach their ideal job. Most of us will need to acquire a collection of professional experiences to get where we want. Cliff Hakim said it best in his book: *We Are All Self-Employed*, the path to progress is more of a "lattice" than a "ladder". As shown below, there are many benefits to a lattice compared to the ladder:

THINK CAREER LATTICE, NOT CAREER LADDER

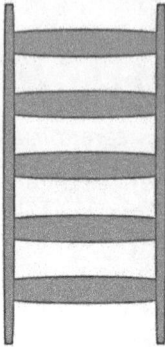

VICE
PRESIDENT

SALES
MANAGER

ACCOUNT
MANAGER

ASSOCIATE
SALES REP

JUNIOR
SALES REP

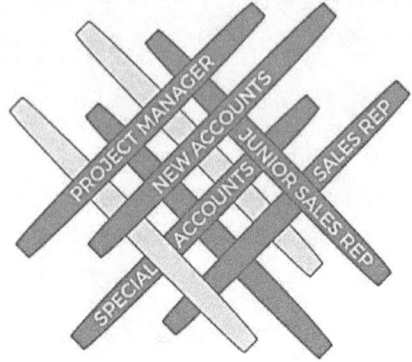

CAREER LADDER

CAREER LATTICE

Career Lattice graphic courtesy of www.NJBobro.com,
NJ Bobro Career Coaching and Consulting

LADDER	LATTICE
Limited Paths to Success	Multiple Paths to Success
Limited Mobility	High Mobility
Hierarchical	Matrixed
Independent	Collaborative
Tasks Define Work	Competencies Define Work
Coworkers are Similar	Coworkers are Different
Linear Career Path	Multidirectional Career Path
Individual Contributor	Team Member

Many of us are puzzled when we leave school because we don't have a clear path. But pathways, ladders and lattices become clearer through self-education, observation, volunteering and networking with others in professions where we have interest.

We are all self-employed. We are responsible for managing our brand inside and outside of our company. We are measured by our own social media pages and the comments we make on the social media pages of others. Post mindfully. Post with the idea that your current or potential employer will be reviewing your words beyond your resume in order to help with their hiring decision.

We are all self-employed: We are responsible for managing our brand inside and outside of our company.

We live in an "at will" nation; this means that the employer or employee may terminate their relationship with each other for any reason. Most employees are not legally bound to stay with an employer and most employers are not legally bound to keep employees. Another consideration of managing our brands: social media. According to The Recruiter Network, a Jobvite Study revealed that:

- **92% of Recruiters are using social media to make hiring decisions**
- 87% of recruiters are vetting candidates through LinkedIn
- 55% vet candidates through Facebook
- 47% check Twitter accounts
- 3% use SnapChat
- The remainder use Periscope, Vimeo, and Tumblr [2]

Create a Career Brand: These are Your Aspirations and What You Want Others to Buy

Ask yourself three questions:

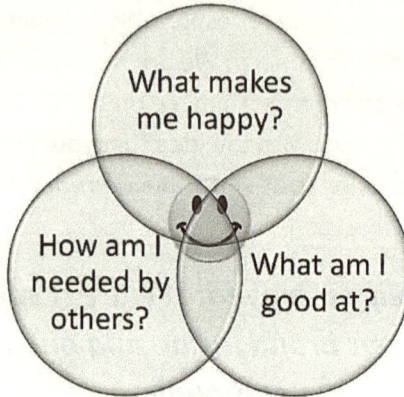

At the intersection of each of these three questions inside the circles is YOUR brand. When you are managing your career by following your brand, energy is focused on finding roles and working on projects where you can thrive. More importantly, your work doesn't feel like labor because you are doing what you love. When you are engaged at work and accomplishing goals according to your brand, it's called "flow state", or some call it "being in the zone." We are fully immersed in what we are doing, and we only realize what time it is because we are either hungry, or it's dark outside.

How does this help me find a job?

Managing your career is the first step in managing your job search. If you know what your interests and career goals are, it will be much easier to know which jobs are a fit for you. By fit, we mean something you and your employer will benefit from, AND contributes to you making positive progression on your career path. Here are some questions to consider periodically to make sure you stay on track:

- What are my career goals?
- What knowledge, skills and experiences will I need to achieve my goals?
- What do I need in order to improve my personal brand?
- What projects will help me achieve my goals?
- How are my assignments/projects helping me to achieve my career goals?

When the interviewer asks you why you are the right person for the job, you'll be ready to provide an honest, meaningful answer because you've taken the first step at documenting what is important to you and how it aligns with their needs.

When I find a career role ("job"), how can I get noticed?

- Be results-driven.
- Demonstrate steady, self-improvement.
- Make sure leaders know you by name.
- Focus your time on results, not on being busy.
- Ask to be put on special project teams.
- Have honest conversations, but don't hurt people's feelings.
- Add value. If you don't know how you're adding value, ask how your project will be measured and how leaders will measure success.
- Politely challenge the status quo with an improvement agenda.
- When you find a problem, consider two or three ways of solving it; then talk to your supervisor about how you want to help.

What do I do when I want to apply for a new job within my company or NEED to find a new job because my company asked me to leave?

The goal of this book is to equip you with the tools you will need for multiple career moves during your lifetime of employment. Most of us will have at least 12 different roles before we retire. Every time we move from one role to another, we will be:

- Networking
- Updating our resume
- Preparing for the interview
- Negotiating
- Onboarding ourselves to ensure success

> **This book provides tools and techniques to help you succeed. Most of you will need these skills at least 12 times over the lifetime of your career.**

Introduction

"If you don't know where you are going, any road will take you there."
—Cheshire Cat, Alice's Adventures in Wonderland

What do most people do when conducting their job search? Most people start flooding the job search engines with resumes (Indeed, Simply Hired, LinkedIn, etc.), blindly responding to ads where hundreds if not thousands of people are expressing interest electronically at the same time. If you are lucky, you are one of the few resumes that are nearly a 100% match to the Applicant Tracking System. Yes, your resume is being instantly screened by your prospective employer, rapidly and neatly sifting through non-matches, placing yours and thousands of others' resumes in a virtual electronic trash bin, never to be seen by a recruiter or hiring manager.

You need a strategy, period. These are the most common strategies job-seekers tend to use, but they are the least effective:

- **Search Firm**
- **Headhunter**
- **Employment Agency**
- **Advertisement**

According to an article published by CNBC, "70% of all jobs are not published on publicly available job search sites...and 50%-80% of jobs are filled through personal and professional connections."[3]

Up to 80% of jobs are filled through networking

The strategies in this book apply to you whether you are employed, under-employed or unemployed. As many as...

70% of jobs are not advertised, so how can you find them? Networking.

So, what was our goal in publishing this book?

Our goal in delivering these strategies is to provide you with a toolkit of resources you need to steer your career in the direction you want regardless of where you are right now.

This book may be read sequentially, chapter-by-chapter, or as an indexed resource. Either read it from the beginning or open the chapter where you need the most help. Then, learn valuable lessons to help you during your planned or unplanned transition.

Managing your career is a life skill, not a luxury. Sure, some people just fall into a dream job, or so they say. Most people get the job of their choice because they know what they want and they are not afraid to go after it. If you do your research, have a plan, and use your resources, you will succeed in finding a job that meets your career goals.

Let's face it, some people have their dream job and will stay in that job for the remainder of their career, but in reality, even during historically low unemployment[4]:

> **Over 80% of Full-time Workers are Actively Seeking or Passively Open to New Job Opportunities**

◆◆◆

After reading the book, post a question on **LinkedIn** if you have a specific question you would like answered.
https://www.linkedin.com/company/consulting-helps/

Remember to "follow" us to see other questions and thread responses to critical career questions.

Contact us if you would like to have Jim and Brant join a conference, meeting or classroom as guest speakers. We are available for one-on-one coaching and instruction. Visit our web site to learn more at:
www.ConsultingHELPSYou.com

Email us at JimandBrant@ConsultingHELPSYou.com

Join our mailing list to receive email alerts when downloadable content, templates and new books become available.

Chapter 1: Career Story Development

Ryan: New to Job Market/Recent Graduate

"Can this week get any worse?" Ryan yelled at no one in particular as his voice echoed in the empty kitchen. Earlier this week he got an email from the dean telling the graduating class of 2020 that they would have a 'virtual' graduation, but to not worry, because at 'some point later' they will be able to walk the stage if they choose. And now his offer of employment with Omega has been "rescinded due to dramatic company restructuring". With exasperation in his voice, he once again posed questions to an empty room, "Now what am I going to do?" *I have done everything right! Everything was going according to plan, now this.* Ryan thought. *When is life going to get back to normal?*

Christine, his mom, was listening from the other room while working from her makeshift home office that doubles as a craft room. Ryan affectionately calls it her 'She-Shed'. She herself has asked that same question every day for the last month. Her big project was set to kick off two weeks ago and now everything is on hold. On top of that, her boss just told her that she would have to lay off 50% of her staff and ask the others if they would be willing to work a 50% reduced schedule until things get back to normal. That is 12 people's lives that she is about to change at just about the worst possible time in her memory.

Christine's 22-year-old son, Ryan, was about to graduate and enter the job market. He is already jumping into a specialized field, but now, with unemployment numbers hitting record highs Christine knows Ryan is going to have to be well-prepared to get noticed by hiring managers. On top of that, her husband was just asked to leave his company of 15 years. *What will the new normal look like? How are we going to make that happen?* She thought. That might be the better question she mumbled to her own empty room as she went to check on Ryan.

Christine enters the room and sees Ryan working on his resume at the Kitchen table

Ryan, you've got great skills.

You're just saying that because you're my mom.

Not true young man. Have you ever sat back and reflected on what you have done up to this point in your life and summarized what it was you were actually doing?

I'm not sure I follow you Mom.

Look, it's a simple exercise to get you thinking about your next step. You'll need to do this each time you add more transferable skills to your toolbox throughout your career.

I'm going to make this exercise simple by providing you a list of transferable skills I KNOW you have already acquired.

Okay.

Christine hands Ryan the list

Here you go!

Grocery List

Accountability
Adaptability
Analytical Skills
Business Acumen
Communication
Confidence
Critical Thinking
Customer Service
Digital Literacy
Facilitating
Flexibility
Initiative
Leading
Managing Priorities
Multi-tasking
Negotiating
Organization
Organizing
Ownership
Perseverance
Philanthropy
Planning
Problem Solving
Public Speaking
Resilience
Selling
Teamwork

Ryan reaches for the list as his mom continues to coach him

> I want you to think about everything you have accomplished, everything you have worked on, anything you have participated in as a volunteer, at school, church, in sports, music, during your part-time job, everything!

> Don't put too much thought into it; just put a check next to everything you've done.

> Got it, thanks Mom!

Ryan starts checking items off the list. After missing a few items he goes back as he recollects ALL of his experiences. He soon realizes he's checked off nearly every item on the list.

- ✓ Accountability
- ✓ Adaptability
- ✓ Analytical Skills
- ✓ Business Acumen
- ✓ Communication
- ✓ Confidence
- ✓ Critical Thinking
- ✓ Customer Service
- ✓ Digital Literacy
- ✓ Facilitating
- ✓ Flexibility
- ✓ Initiative
- ✓ Leading
- ✓ Managing Priorities
- ✓ Multi-tasking
- ✓ Negotiating
- ✓ Organization
- ✓ Organizing
- ✓ Ownership
- ✓ Perseverance
- ✓ Philanthropy
- ✓ Planning
- ✓ Problem Solving

- ✓ Public Speaking
- ✓ Resilience
- ✓ Selling
- ✓ Teamwork

Okay.

Ryan rests his pen on the table next to the list and Christine starts to examine the list over his shoulder

That's a good start. Now let's read one of those jobs you are interested in.

You mean from Simply Hired?

Yes.

What does that have to do with this, Mom?

Landing a job you want is all about alignment Ryan. Not only does the Applicant Tracking System need to see that you have the skills to get the job done, it will also screen for HOW you are capable of getting the job done. Just humor me for a minute.

Ryan somewhat frustrated rolls his eyes

Okay. Here is that job I was telling you about the other day.

Christine stares at the screen next to Ryan

Let's read through it together. As we are reading, which skills do you see in the job description match the items you have checked from the grocery list of skills?

There are four, wait five that are a perfect match.

Good. Now before you are ready to talk to someone about why you're a good candidate for the job, you need to have a good story to tell. In this case, I want you to develop at least five stories, one story for each of the items you checked on your list that matches the job description you have in front of you.

Before you are ready to talk to someone about why you're a good candidate for the job, you need to have a good story to tell.

Why not just tell them during the interview?

That's my point.

The problem with the interview process is that not all employers have qualified people conducting the interview. In order to give you an advantage over the competition, you need to be prepared to share your story and structured in a way that the interviewer sees you as someone that is qualified for the job.

The problem with the interview process is that not all employers have qualified people conducting the interview. In order to give you a leg up on the competition, you need to be prepared to share your story and structured in a way that the interviewer sees you as someone that is qualified for the job.

Ryan looking puzzled

A structured way?

Yes, through storytelling. We want your stories to help uniquely position you among other job candidates so you stand out. Good stories answer questions like: Why? What? When? Where? and How? *explained Christine*

Storytelling....Good stories answer questions like Why? What? When? Where? and How?

I want you to follow an acronym when creating each of your stories, it's called **SCORE**.

SCORE

Scope – What was I faced with? What was the problem I had to solve? What would happen if the problem wasn't addressed?

Chore – What was assigned to me? What was I responsible for managing or completing?

Obstacles – What challenges was I faced with, and how did I overcome them and solve the problem?

Results – How did I achieve the desired results? What were the measurable results? What were the short and long-term impacts on efficiency, effectiveness, cost savings and cost avoidance?

Evaluate – What did I learn during the process?

Thanks Mom, I think I get it now. This is going to take me some time. Would you mind having a look at what I came up with after putting pen to paper?

Of course Ryan, I'm here to help.

What about my resume? Shouldn't I make sure my stories are reflected there too?

Absolutely! But for your resume, you want to highlight the measurable accomplishments that align with your stories. The pitfall most people fall into when writing their resumes is listing the tasks they have performed, but fail to write the results.

The pitfall most people fall into when writing their resumes is listing the tasks they have performed, but failing to write the results.

Your resume is an advertisement to get the person reading it to want more.

Finish your stories first; then we can circle back and make sure every one of your stories has a measurable result. Then, we can add the measurable results to your resume to help grab the reader's attention.

Add the measurable results to your resume to help grab the reader's attention.

NOTE: Please visit the Appendix section *Turning Contributions into Numbers* for inspiration and ideas on measurable results you can add to your resume.

So Ryan, how did you decide this job is right for you?

Ryan thumbs through his notebook

Well, I did a simple analysis using a four-box model one of my teachers used to share with us at school to help analyze problems and make decisions. I modified it to determine my current skills on one axis and my level of interest on the other axis.

	Learning /	**Career**
	Growth	**Storytelling**
	Opportunity	**Match**
	Express enthusiasm to learn new skill and leverage transferrable skills.	Share how you have done this in the past and how you can hit the ground running!
	Red Flag / Poor Match	**Boredom / Second Nature**
	Avoid opportunities where the majority (60% or more) of the job falls into this quadrant.	Consider avoiding unless the job only requires a small percentage of your skills in this quadrant.

Vertical axis: Interest

Horizontal axis: Skill

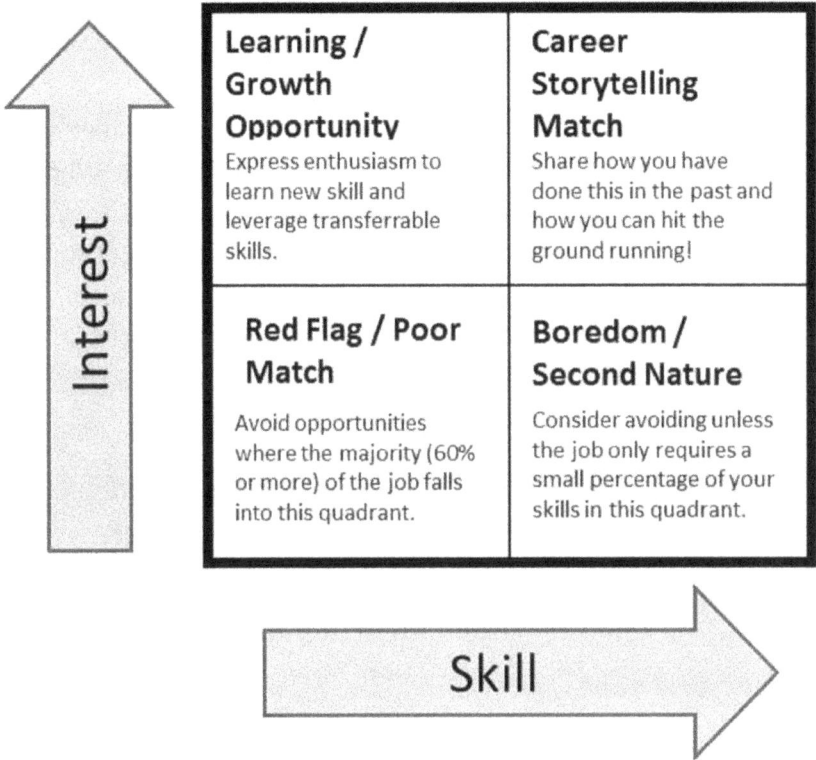

I have figured out that this job opportunity will allow me to hit the ground running with a handful of my existing skills that they are looking for, while at the same time provide me with ample opportunity for learning and growth in my career.

What if the job is asking for a skill I don't have yet?

With a smirk on her face, Christine coaches Ryan

I can't believe I'm answering this question in this way, but 'Google' it, 'YouTube' it. Just because you don't have experience doesn't mean you can't educate yourself on what they need. There are countless links to resources to help teach you what you need to know.

Ryan, still confused

But what about experience?

Depending on what you need to learn for a role in your career, you may have all the experience you need by being self-taught. When you're asked by the interviewer how you learned this skill, they will be silly not to hire you after showing so much initiative. But you don't want to pretend to be an expert. Be honest and let them know what you've learned and how you are looking forward to learning more while applying your skills in a professional environment.

Transferable Skills: Be honest and let them know what you've learned and how you are looking forward to applying your skills in a professional environment.

Ryan letting out a sigh of relief

I get it now, thanks Mom.

I guess you have more of a handle on this than I had expected. Let me know when you're ready for me to review those stories.

Chapter 2: Networking Strategy

Ken: Experienced Leader

Ken (Christine's husband)

Sitting in the President's office Friday afternoon

"Ken...we had to reduce every VP's severance package due to the tough times the company has been facing over the past several months. Instead of 1 year, now it's 8 months", stated the president of the company.

Ken really didn't comprehend the rest of the conversation, it felt more like it was happening to someone else and he was just watching from afar. The representative from HR was in the room and said a few things about insurance and such, but stated that everything was in this packet, which she handed over to him.

He remembered turning in the keys to the company car, which he hated to give up and they told him to go ahead and go home via the Uber Black that they had arranged. "Don't worry" they said and that they'll get all his personal effects boxed up and sent to him.

I haven't looked for a job in 25 years! Ken blurted out to the empty back seat.

The Uber driver chimed in

> The last guy I took home after getting laid off had me stop at the
>
> liquor store, would you like for me to do the same?

Ken thought about it for a second and a gin and tonic did sound pretty good right about now

> Sure.

After a brief stop at the store, he realized that he couldn't even give his wife, Christine, a heads up on what happened because he didn't have a phone! She'll find out soon enough once he steps out of the black town car carrying a bottle of gin.

Where's your car?

Well, Honey, I'm on the other side of the wall now.

Christine just noticed the cardboard banker's box Ken was carrying. The lid on the box flapping in the wind and the only thing keeping it from closing was a tall bottle of Beefeater, her favorite gin. Christine smiling with an impish tone in her voice.

Were you drinking at work?

Ha, Ha, Ha...you know me better than that. Maybe I should have been drinking and given them a real reason to fire me! It was nothing like that.

Ken continues to talk as he brings Christine up to speed while walking into the house.

The company has been going through a tough time. We just haven't been hitting our numbers for several quarters. Our products aren't competing with what is now available on the global market so the Board of Directors decided it was in the best interest of our stockholders to sell our division. Who wants to hire a 55+ year-old man with 25 years of experience?

We both know what you need to do. There's no sense toiling over it right now. Let's have dinner. I've been working with Ryan on some of the basics and he's taken his knowledge to help his friend Chip. You're in a slightly different situation, but I think we'll start with the basics; then put a plan together so you can ride out the last years before we head into retirement.

As Ken was unpacking his banker's box and getting changed before dinner, he reflected on how quickly the last 8 years had passed. He really thought his last job would be his 'last' job. Why me? Why now? Fortunately, Ryan had graduated from college, so there was one less expense that had to be managed.

Thank you for dinner Honey, great job as usual.

Ken and Christine spent some time brainstorming next steps. Both agreed that his main focus should be on networking since the majority of jobs filled in the market are not advertised. After a few phone calls Ken felt he would be picked up by a new company in no time and have a chance to collect a paycheck and his severance at the same time. But that never happened. Two weeks of promises seemingly evaporated and now Ken has been out of the market for three months. He realizes now just calling people he remembers hasn't paid off as planned.

The main focus when seeking a new job should be <u>NETWORKING,</u> since the majority of jobs filled in the market are not advertised.

Ryan walks into the home office where Ken is working on his next step.

How's it going Dad?

It's going okay, how about you Son?

I've got my foot in the door with a new company. My online orientation program starts Monday. After that, I'll go onsite for an in-person orientation and start learning about my new role. You seem a little off Dad, is everything okay?

Well, I'm glad to hear you're getting some traction in your career. You have many great years ahead of you and honestly, I'm a little jealous. I'm at a different stage in my career. It's tough finding my next spot since there are so few opportunities for people with my experience.

What have you been doing in your search strategy up to this point?

For me, it's all about networking. Networking is one letter away from 'not working'; don't you forget that. It's a valuable skill you can take advantage of inside and outside the company where you're working. I feel like I've hit a wall.

Networking is one letter away from NOT Working

There are at least five different types of networking contacts we have in our lives.

Contact Type	Description
Social	Friends and family
Personal	Serve a special purpose and we are less likely to introduce them to others
Professional	Allies, coaches, mentors and mentees
Collegial	Peers, bosses, clients and vendors
Tactical	Influencers, seed-planters, project sponsors

Ryan leaning over his Dad's shoulder and looking at his computer screen

What does your LinkedIn profile look like, and how are you taking advantage of making connections using online resources?

Well, I haven't really gotten into the whole social media thing. Maybe I should?

You'd be surprised how many people are on social media, even people your age...no offense. Your LinkedIn profile is almost like a virtual resume or curriculum vitae. You have the opportunity to connect with people in companies where you've worked and make new contacts within companies you may be interested in joining. It's an opportunity to advertise to others how you can help. There are also communities you can join based on your expertise and interests.

Social media has given us new tools to connect with others. These tools can be leveraged to stay in touch with people we know and to make new contacts. Networking is about establishing relationships with other people that share common interests. What makes a good networking contact? Ask yourself some questions:

1. **Do I like this person?**
2. **Does this person seem to like me?**
3. **Do I think I can help this person?**
4. **Can I see this person helping me?**
5. **When we talk, do I like what I hear?**

If you answered 'Yes' to at least three of these questions, you have established a viable networking contact.

Have you ever 'Googled' yourself Dad?

I can't say that I have, what would be the point in doing that?

When you have a LinkedIn profile and someone 'Googles' you, your LinkedIn profile is likely the first thing to show up, and you WANT that to happen. If you don't have a LinkedIn profile, potential employers may question your professional aptitude. The great thing about LinkedIn is that it is always available for anyone that wants to use it and it's focused solely on professionals. It's not just another social media platform. *Ryan shares excitedly*

Ken nodded with interest

Anyone serious about their career has a complete profile on LinkedIn.

I feel like I've been missing something. What are the top 10 things I should do to have a great LinkedIn profile?

I think we're going to have to call Mom in to check my answers on this, but here is what I've learned by building my profile on LinkedIn and helping to get noticed:

1. **What's your story?** Reflect on your accomplishments and turn them into stories.
2. **Headlines** - Take the essence of your stories and turn them into headlines to get people interested in meeting the real you.
3. **Take a good profile picture**, NOT like the bland headshot photo on your driver's license - it's how we make a first impression when people find us online.
4. **Action Verbs** - Use Action Verbs to best describe you and your accomplishments.
5. **Skills: What you bring to the table!** Add all your relevant skills; others in your network will then be asked to rate whether or not you have this skill - it's worth reaching out to a few folks and have them rate your skills. We want you to look good!
6. **Connect with people** - Dust off your contact list and find people you know. Connect with them on LinkedIn, then find out what groups they belong to and join those groups to grow your professional presence.

7. **Follow companies** where you have an interest. This will provide you with alerts and posts from companies of interest to keep you current with what is going on in the industry. It will also help you when researching companies.
8. **Ask for recommendations** - Reach out to former peers, colleagues and bosses to get them to tell the world how great you are. Have THEM share a brief story of the impact you had at the company, on a project or during a unique situation
9. **Show Your Work** - remember math? The only time we get credit in math class is to show our work. Include links to some of your publications or speaking engagements.
10. **Join Groups and Be Active** - There is a group for every interest, profession and career level on LinkedIn. It's also important to share content and opinions with others in your professional community.

Okay, I'm on LinkedIn now. I found someone that I know but it won't let me send them a message, what now?

We need to build your profile first. After you've built your profile, which is kind of like an online resume, all the companies where you've worked will be linked to your profile, which will allow you to send messages to others that have worked for that same company.

What's the 'Premium' service offer?

LinkedIn Premium increases your visibility in search results by recruiters and in job applications

The Premium membership allows you to directly contact a number of people outside of your network each month. I'd suggest signing up for the free trial. See if you like it; then you can pay the monthly subscription to keep it going.

So can I use LinkedIn to connect with people I already know?

Of course. Even better, you can use your existing contact list from your email to see people you know that are already on LinkedIn and invite hundreds of people to connect with you all at once. Don't forget, you also want to click the button to tell others you are 'Actively Applying' for jobs as this will help recruiters know you are seeking and not just passively looking.

I can't believe I've waited this long to get caught up with technology. I guess one of my greatest weaknesses is that I immerse myself in my role. I worked for that company for so many years that I really lost track of many of the people I had worked with up to that point. It will be good to get reconnected.

Ryan smirked

Good talk Dad. We'll do this again soon.

So when you have all these people in your virtual network on LinkedIn, then what?

Ryan looked back at his Dad with a quizzical look on his face

You see, it's not about how many virtual relationships you have that means you have a solid network. These are real people. Think about accomplishing the FEAT of networking.

Networking is a daily, weekly and monthly FEAT when you are helping others and they are helping you.

FEAT

Find them and follow-up — either directly or through an introduction.

Engage with them by discussing and sharing information that meets their interests and needs.

Appreciate genuinely the time you spend with each other—this is not a task to be impatiently rushed.

Thank them for their time and find opportunities to help them.

Thank you Son, I really appreciate your help.

I think we both learned something here Dad. Networking really IS one letter away from **not working**.

Chapter 3: Networking Execution

Joel: Experienced Professional

NETworking is one letter away from NOT Working

Let's look at a few statistics based on generations in the workplace

- **59% of Gen Z would expect to stay with their current employer for less than 2 years (Deloitte)[5]**

- **50% of Millennials say 1-2 years is the right length of time to stay in a job before looking for another (Ajilon)[6]**

- **66% of Gen X'ers received just ONE promotion, or NONE AT ALL (AARP)[7]**

Not all of us will be asked to leave one of our 12 careers over a lifetime. But what's worse than being asked to leave? How about being miserable, day after day and doing nothing about it. The key to success is networking. Let's visit with Joel and find out more about how he will take his next step.

Walking to the car carrying a box of family pictures and knick-knacks along with about 30 other coworkers, or now ex coworkers, doing the exact same thing, Joel was struggling to accept what just happened. Almost 20 years of experience, multiple awards, a Senior leadership position, several credentials, an MBA, now what? Joel is always loyal to his employers and especially this one. He really thought this was the company that would be his last and bid him farewell into retirement.

Talking to no one in particular, Joel says, "I guess I'll be entering the job market with about 1 million other workers across the state." Sitting in the car, he just stared straight ahead looking at the building he had been coming to for the past 7 years, wondering where he would go tomorrow...and the next day. Why did this have to happen? Why now? About that time the phone rang, and he looked at the caller ID and took a deep breath. This was the conversation he had been dreading.

Cell phone ringing.

His wife's smiling face was on the caller id screen. How was he going to tell his wife what had happened while trying not to sound upset? She worked part time at the local pre-school, that way she could take care of the kids and still earn a little money. But now, with 5 mouths to feed and no severance package, things will be tough, to say the least. He put on his best fake smile and pushed the green button.

Hi Honey...how's it going?

I'm fine dear, what time do you think you'll be home tonight for dinner, the kids are starving!

Well, I'll be home a little early tonight. Need me to pick anything up at the grocery?

No, we are all set. Don't forget we have our mentoring group with the parish tonight.

I remember...all the more reason to get home early and get ready for the evening.

Joel and Lois have been active mentors in their place of worship for some time now. They have grown quite a loyal following over the years and have only recently been teaching others how to succeed in the job market.

Unbeknownst to Joel, this is a 'network'. Joel probably never viewed this group he and Lois facilitated every month to be a group he would depend on for help, but selflessly he probably assumed the only role he and Lois played with this group was to give help, not ask for anything in return. This was all about to change.

Glad you're home early, Honey, what's wrong? Something happen at work today?

You may say that. Today was my last day. I'm shocked. I feel lost. I invested so many years with that company just to be let go. And based on the current market, the whole company could go under. I guess I'm lucky because even though I didn't get a severance package, I was able to negotiate that the company pay our health insurance for the next six months. Others may not be so lucky.

Lois took a deep breath and a minute to process what she just heard. So many of her friends have heard something similar over the past few months and she had often wondered how she would handle the news, now she was about to see if she could react the way she wanted.

Giving Joel a hug that they both needed

It will be okay. Well, good thing we have our session tonight so you can start your networking campaign.

But most of these people don't work in my industry.

That's not the point of networking, Honey. Networking is about connecting with those around you, then meeting with other people, getting the word out, and finding out how you can each help each other.

Networking is about connecting with those around you, talking to people about meeting with other people, getting the word out, and finding out how you can each help each other.

I guess you're right.

Haven't you learned by now that I'm always right? *She joked*. I've worked in Business Development for years. I know you're not a networker by trade, you like going to the office and getting yourself immersed in work. Let's come up with a marketing strategy for you starting with networking.

I need to get my resume out there and start applying for jobs, Lois. I don't have time to be making a bunch of phone calls.

You're missing the point. Most people get hired by word-of-mouth networking and filling positions that may or may not be advertised to the public. Networking gives you an edge over the thousands of people blindly submitting resumes.

When we get home I want you to do the following:

1. **First,** create a list of everyone you know.
    a. Classmates
    b. Friends
    c. Families (immediate and extended)
    d. Community Outreach/Volunteer relationships
    e. Religious Groups (Churches, Temples, Synagogues, and Mosques)
    f. Alumni
    g. Teachers/Professors
    h. Colleagues (current and former)
    i. Bosses/Supervisors/Managers
    j. Trade Association contacts

2. **Second,** put a check mark next to every person's name you believe will pick up the phone. You'll call everyone on the list eventually, but start with the checked names.
3. **Third,** start smilin' and dialin', Honey!

Why not just log into my LinkedIn account or my Indeed account and start sending resumes to posted jobs?

You can, but first check your network. There is a whole other set of steps I can run through quickly for you:

1. **First, if you see a job you like, check your network first.** Find out on LinkedIn how connected you are to someone within that organization. Try to get the name of a real person before blindly emailing a resume or submitting your interest through a job board on LinkedIn, Indeed or some other platform. Most companies offer employees referral bonuses for getting you in the door.
2. **Second, reach out to people in your network.** Get connected to a real person within that company. If you don't see anyone in your network, call the company directly and ask to speak to someone to learn more about the job. Networked contacts can help provide an easier introduction to the hiring manager (check their LinkedIn profile as many professionals list their email address). Then, ask for the name of the manager for whichever department you're interested in joining.
3. **Third, fine-tune the resume you want to submit for the job.** I know you have a dusty old resume out there somewhere, but today's job seeker needs to fine tune their resume for **EACH** job they are applying for. Lord knows we don't have enough paper to have everything we've ever done published on a resume, that's why they should all be aligned before applying.

a. **Update** your resume with responsibilities, tasks and projects that align with the prospective role.

b. Have your resume **proofread** by someone else, not you! Email and phone numbers must be exactly right today since many Applicant Tracking Systems have programs that work on a Chabot/text platform to automatically keep candidates updated on progress.

c. Some jobs provide the opportunity to include a **cover letter**. Create something that grabs the reader's attention so they know what makes you unique and how you can add value.

4. **Fourth, apply for the job. If Steps 1 and 2 didn't work,** apply directly on the company's website to make sure you are in the company's Applicant Tracking System.

5. **Finally, follow-up.** If you were lucky enough to get the name of a person within the company, call them one to two weeks after applying to find out what the status is of the interview process.

What if I can't find anyone connected to the company?

That's when it's time to get creative, Honey. You need to go onto LinkedIn and search for the person in the company you think you'll be reporting to, then call the company and get that person on the phone. Even if they don't answer the phone, leave a voicemail to let them know you are interested in helping them fill that role because you're an ideal fit. Help them understand the value you can bring based on your experience.

Also, according to a report I heard on National Public Radio (NPR), most jobs aren't posted or advertised publicly. A lot of jobs only appear internally at companies because most companies have policies that require them to first try and hire from within.

But when the company doesn't have enough competent people to hire or promote into vacant roles, they reach out to the job market. Your goal is to get noticed AFTER the company realizes they need to find someone and BEFORE the company makes that job public. NPR says that at least 70% of jobs are not published on job boards like Indeed, LinkedIn, Simply Hired or Monster.

Most job openings within companies aren't posted or advertised publicly. A lot of jobs only appear internally at companies because most companies want to hire from within. Then, they are advertised AFTER the company cannot find a suitable candidate internally or through networking.

I think I'm starting to get it now, Lois. Networking IS one letter away from Not Working.

Remember, networking is one letter away from 'NOT Working'

When you are networking with people, make sure you ask them for the names of two or three other people that would be good for you to talk to. Here is how you should ask:

Good: Who are two or three people that would be good for me to talk to and continue learning more?

Bad: Do you know two or three people that would want to talk to me?

Do you see the difference between those two questions?

1. The first question is 'open', it's not making it easy for the person you are speaking with to answer with a yes or no.

2. The second question is closed, so the person you are speaking with can EASILY answer yes or no.

I get it Lois, thank you for the advice. Now it's time for me to start smilin' and dialin'!

Chapter 4: Resume (Part I)
Heather: Experienced Manager

Fun fact: Leonardo da Vinci is credited with sending the first "resume", which comes from the French word of the same spelling meaning: summary. He had written a letter in the late 1400s to a potential employer, Ludovico Sforza.[8]

Heather tried to hide her frustration on the Zoom call, but it was no use. While working virtually, person-to-person sales calls were a thing of the past. She had been traveling throughout North America for the past few years. Occasionally, she visited her larger international clients, collecting data to create reports that help guide her clients' decisions.

But now everything has changed. Her clients were laying off large numbers of their staff and a few clients even filed for bankruptcy, owing her company sizable sums of money for the software packages she sold them, and many were cancelling the monthly services. So when her boss scheduled the Zoom call for Friday after lunch, she had a feeling that something bad was coming.

Heather had expected this call several weeks earlier, she knew the numbers just weren't adding up, so she had started coming to terms with a possible layoff and started planning how she was going to get through it. She cut back on going out and decided she didn't need all those things in her Amazon shopping cart. She even began sending emails to some contacts she hadn't talked to in a while that were in her field.

On the phone call earlier, her boss said all the right things, but when the company is struggling to make payroll, what can you do? She didn't need the sugar-coating, just get to the point she thought to herself. She smiled politely and thanked her boss for the opportunity and that when they got back up and running to give her a call, He told her "you'll be the first I call back". Well, thought Heather, time to get to how to best go about her next project and get back to work. Right now her job is finding the next role to pay the bills and keep on her career path.

Heather, thinking to herself, I've always focused my stories around what I accomplished and the data and financial results of my projects. With so many qualified candidates in the market today, it's even more important to differentiate myself by explaining HOW I work effectively as an individual and my contributions as a team member, but not just talking about WHAT I've done.

> **With so many qualified candidates in the market today, it's even more important to differentiate yourself by explaining HOW you work effectively (independently, on a team or leading others) and not just WHAT you've done.**

Cell phone chime...incoming text

L

Hi Lois, long time no speak.

Heather!!! It has been too long, are you still pulling down those big contracts like the old days?

Well, the market the past several quarters has pushed all of us to the bottom of the leaderboard I'm afraid.

You and me both!

I'm on the other side of the wall now Lois, looking for my next big opportunity.

I'm sorry to hear that Heather, this market has been tough on everyone. Just the other day Joel was let go and on the other side as well. What can I do to help?

L

That's why I called you, I knew you would be one of the first people to respond!

I'm happy to help. What did you have in mind?

I'm really looking for help on updating my resume. You were always good at drafting the biographies that we sent to our clients.

Email me a copy of your current resume. Meanwhile, take some time to write down all of your key accomplishments in your career. I know you're a numbers person like me, so make sure to drop some of those seven-figure contracts you pulled in while we were working together; just make a list. Then we'll get together to take your data and my recommendations to build you a world-class resume!

L

Okay, I just hit the send button. Talk soon.

Your resume is only part of the story. How prepared are you to talk about how YOU have the attributes THEY want in a candidate?

Tell me more

Most companies on their websites, in their mission statements and written into their values, tell you what kind of person can be successful. There are dozens of desirable attributes companies want in a candidate, but if you don't have them in your resume or can't articulate them in the interview, you'll be passed over for a candidate that is better at telling their story.

Hmmmmm

L

You mean like "Teamwork?"

Exactly! Along with Teamwork, I'm going to suggest six more that nearly every company wants to see during the hiring process. An important one is passion! I know you are passionate and have a hunger for this kind of work – I'll work with you to make sure that comes across to whoever is reading your resume.

Thank you Lois!!!

Check your inbox. I just emailed your homework assignment so we can get your resume noticed!

I know you Heather and you're very good at details, the data, and working with people. When you incorporate those attributes in your resume and by sharing real stories of your experience during the interview, the hiring manager would be foolish to hire someone else.

Heather,

Here are the attributes that every company wants in their team members (including Teamwork!). I got this list from a recruiter friend of mine years ago, but it's still relevant today. Reflect on your experiences like we talked about, and see how we can incorporate them into your new resume.

Talk soon,

Lois

Attitude - you need to demonstrate that you have a positive attitude regardless of situations you have faced in your career.

Passion - this is that 'hunger' I mentioned before, you need to show you are anxious to join the team and help out by applying your unique skills.

Self-Motivated - if you can't get across to the recruiter that you are driven by the role you are applying for, the recruiter will see this immediately in the interview and look for another candidate.

Honesty & Integrity - companies don't want people that take shortcuts; shortcuts can get people hurt or killed. Dishonesty can kill a company's social presence or brand.

Adaptability / Change-Adoption Mindset - as companies evolve in shorter periods of time, we need people that are flexible, adept at changing, and resilient , in order to grow personally and help the company grow.

Problem Solving - companies don't hire people because they want their managers and leaders solving employee problems. You need to be perceived as a solution-provider.

Recruiters and companies want career-seekers, not job finders.

Chapter 5: Interviewing

Chip: Young Professional

I can't believe I've only been with this company for 18 months and now I have a shot at a decent promotion, Chip thought to himself. Right out of university, Chip joined the firm and was quickly taken under the wing of a senior associate. Chip's easy-going nature made it easy for him to fit into any client and social situation. His bosses and peers appreciated his spontaneity and, most of all, his ability to get things done quickly.

If I can make a great impression during the interviews, I should be in a great position compared to any external candidate the firm wants to bring in for this role. Fortunately, even if the position is given to another person that is more qualified, at least the higher-ups will know Chip is serious about moving up in the organization.

Ryan and Chip went to school together; both of them were in the band together but were a year apart. Chip landed a role in a company right out of school and right now the two are catching up over coffee.

I'm really interested in this posting, Ryan.

What interests you most about it?

Well, it really fits in those top two quadrants of that four-box model you showed me. It's a great learning opportunity and some of my existing skills can help me hit the ground running!

What concerns do you have about applying for the job?

Well, I want to position myself so my company sees that I'm the best candidate for the role, but interviews have always intimidated me.

Contrary to popular belief, interviewing is not an interrogation. Interviewing is a two-way dialog. The interviewer is asking targeted questions to dive deeper into finding out if you are capable of meeting the needs of the job based on your behavior during past experiences. *Said Ryan*

> **Contrary to popular belief, interviewing is not an interrogation. Interviewing is a two-way dialog. The interviewer wants to know if you are capable of meeting the needs of the job based on your behavior during past experiences.**

So how am I supposed to include all that information when responding to questions?

Well, I've been working with my mom on this very topic. She gave me a great acronym to help me remember how to structure my answers in the form of a story. The acronym is **SCORE (*Chapter 1*)**:

Scope – What was I faced with? What was the problem I had to solve? What would happen if the problem weren't addressed?

Chore – What was assigned to me? What was I responsible for managing or completing?

Obstacles – What challenges was I faced with and how did I overcome them to solve the problem?

Results – What were the measurable results? What were the short and long-term impacts on efficiency, effectiveness, cost savings and cost avoidance?

Evaluate – What did I learn during the process?

But how will I know that the story I'm telling is aligned with something they need.

Remember, it's not an interrogation. Look at it this way: an interview is just a business meeting. Your job in the business meeting is to find out what issues they have and their expectations of the person in the role. You need to ask questions and listen for their needs. Their needs, plus your related experiences, equal the key topics of conversation.

> **An interview is just a business meeting. Your job in the business meeting is to find out what issues they have and their expectations. You need to ask questions and listen for their needs; then present your experiences as the solution.**

Okay, I get it! After I figure out their needs, then I can pick which story is best for them to hear so they know I have what they need to hit the ground running!

I think you're getting it now, Chip. Think about it this way:

1. **First**, ask the right questions.
2. **Second**, listen for content and intent.
    a. What are they telling you?
    b. Why is it such an issue for them?
3. **Third, paraphrase what you think you heard**. Inferred communication will not help you here, you need verbal validation that you heard what they meant to tell you, then you can share the right story.

What would be some good questions for me to ask?

Make sure you are asking open-ended questions, questions that aren't easily answered with a 'yes' or 'no'. Here are some of my favorites:

- What was it about my background that interested you in speaking with me today?
    - *Get them to tell you how they think you can help them*
- What qualities will a candidate need to succeed in this role?
    - *Learn what qualities they need, then share examples of how you have demonstrated those qualities in the past*
- What do you think is most challenging about this role?
    - *Share examples of how you have overcome their challenges with stories of past projects*
- What is most rewarding about this role?
    - *Explain why the role is such a great fit*
- What advancement opportunities exist after someone has mastered this role?
    - *Demonstrates your interest in a long-term career*
- What are the top three things the person in this role should accomplish in their first year?
    - *Gather this information and take notes if necessary, this is critical content for a detailed follow-up letter and the start of your 30-60-90 Day plan (See **Chapter 11**)*
- What impact would this role allow the ideal candidate to make?
    - *Shows you're interested in making a real difference. Use follow-up questions to uncover measurable results.*

Where did you learn all this stuff, Ryan? This is gold!

I've been working with my mom, and she has been helping me and my Dad now that he has been between jobs for a little while now too.

What if I'm not sure what the answer to my question means?

Ask a good follow-up question, be honest and say, "Can you tell me more about that?"

I get it, so instead of thinking I just need to provide short answers, this SCORE method can help me tell the story of how I have handled similar situations in the past. Then use follow-up questions to maintain a strong two-way communication of fact finding and solution providing. In this case, my stories are where I will be the solution.

Great summary, Chip. I really appreciate how you summarized what we've talked about. This tells me you are already ready for the interview.

Ryan leans across the table

What about your digital etiquette?

I'm not sure I follow you?

Chances are you aren't going to have a traditional interview in a face-to-face setting, so you'll need to be prepared for a few different scenarios:

1. **Video Interview - Just Words:** One interview I had with an employer was just me talking to a video screen. I was prompted with an interview question on screen; then while looking into the camera, I responded as if I were talking to someone face-to-face. It wasn't easy, but if you've already developed your stories, be ready to respond in the form of a story where possible to make sure the person watching the video gets a good sense of who you are, your excitement and capabilities. While sharing your story, maintain eye contact on one focus point on the camera, just as you would during a live interview. And be sure to provide facial expressions

to communicate your non-verbal interest and engagement.

2. **Video Conference Interview:** Another interview I had in the next round of the process is when I got to speak with a real person on camera. This was tougher than I thought because I wasn't able to easily look at my notes. So in preparation, I would recommend taping little copies of your career stories all around your computer monitor and behind the camera. Make sure you summarize them into bullet points to prompt what you want to say, but you don't want to come off like you're reading off a script.

3. **Phone Interview:** The last interview I had before the end of the interview process was a phone interview. What I liked most about the phone interview is I could look at all of my research I had done on the company. I had all my questions in front of me relevant to the person I was meeting with and I had all of my stories easily accessible. Again, I had to make sure I wasn't reading word-for-word because I wanted to come across as natural and not scripted.

4. **Zoom Panel Interview:** Starting in 2020 many more employees and job seekers are working from home. Rather than travel for interviews, many companies are hosting Zoom meetings with candidates. Be prepared to ask each of the members of the interview panel questions to maintain interest and engagement. Pay attention to the Zoom meeting invitation and try to figure out who else may be on the call. Then, use LinkedIn to learn more about them before the meeting.

> Who knows, you may be only one connection away
> from them on LinkedIn!

I don't have a very good connection on my computer. Did you ever run into any issues with the screen freezing or audio issues and if so, how did you deal with it?

Ryan's eyes lit up

I had the same issue in the video conference interview and realized that my Wi-Fi wasn't strong enough to support audio and video. So I moved my laptop into my Dad's office and connected it to the hard line. Our house is wired with Cat7e, and after I connected using the Ethernet cable my next interview was flawless, no issues with audio or video.

Make sure you run your own test before the interview to see if you run into any issues. You can always Skype me or we can have a Zoom meeting with a few friends to test the bandwidth.

Of course, you can always reach out to your point of contact ahead of the meeting to run an audio and video test prior to the meeting. This is also a great strategy to show your planning skills, hunger for the role and reliability.

Thank you Ryan, this has been insightful. I feel better prepared now.

Chapter 6: Resume (Part II)
Heather: Experienced Manager

Incoming Zoom call on Heather's laptop

Hi Lois, thank you for taking time to go over my resume.

My pleasure Heather, all in a day's work. Let's get right to it. *Lois displays Heather's resume on screen.* There are four things we are going to do in order to get you noticed.

Measurable Results	Every job you feature on your resume should have some measurable results. Your future employer wants to know how you have made an impact.
Tables	Remove all tables and text boxes from your resume because most Applicant Tracking Systems cannot read the content within the table. Sure, it looks nice, but your resume will not be read by a human at first, it has to pass through the Applicant Tracking System first. Simplicity is more important than aesthetics.
Action Verbs	'Responsible For' is not a great way to explain the impact you've had in your roles. Try and use a variety of action verbs (See ***Appendix*** for a list) within each job on your resume and also try not to repeat.
File Format	The format requested of you during the application process is critical. Do not submit a .PDF when the requested format is .TXT or .DOC.

This is great feedback Lois, thank you!

I know you keep track of all your sales numbers. I know you called it your 'Bible,' not sure we can call it that anymore, but anyway, your sales journal has all the details you need to build your resume. Use all those big numbers you reeled in as headlines on your resume bullets; then be prepared to share your stories during the interview process to land your next role.

What about my resume objective?

Wow! It really has been a long time since you've crafted a resume, hasn't it?

What structure would you recommend?

Most people want to present what is known as a Functional Resume, and it's structured like this:

1. Name
2. Contact Information
    a. Address
    b. Email
    c. Mobile Phone Number
3. Background/Skills Summary/Technical and Specialized Skills
4. Work Experience (most recent first)
    a. Company Name
    b. Job Title
    c. Dates of Employment
    d. Summary of Accomplishments (Optional)
        • Result 1, starting with an action verb
        • Result 2, starting with an action verb
        • Result 3, starting with an action verb
5. Education
6. Professional Memberships/Licenses/Associations/Professional Certifications

I'm worried about some gaps in my employment when I was in transition. How can I fix my resume to tell a better story?

Instead of using the exact start and end date of every position, just list the years you were in each role, which should help.

Instead of using the exact start and end date of every position, just list the years you were in each role, this helps clean the resume and softens obvious gaps in employment.

Some of the companies I've worked for have gone under, or the department I worked in was restructured shortly after starting. What do I do about that?

It's easy, just add something in parenthesis next to the company name, like "Company Closure" or "Department Reorganization", or in this case, "Reduction in Workforce". This will alert the reader of the resume your short tenure was not something you could control.

Let employers know right on your resume why you left a position, especially if it was out of your control. Add "Company Closure" or "Reduction in Force" in parenthesis somewhere in your resume.

Chapter 7: Tackling Tough Interview Questions

Sam: Experienced Professional

I've been at the top of my game for years, Sam thought to herself. Is now a great time to make a move? A top engineer at her company, Sam found the work just wasn't as challenging or exciting as it used to be. She landed this role because she stayed in touch with her boss at her last firm. Sam didn't mind her current role, but it wasn't the same as when she started. When Sam first joined the firm, they were just starting to grow their engineering team. She had an opportunity to join a new and growing team and soon was regarded as the firm's top engineer.

Retirement is still several years away for Sam, and she realized that if she is going to make a move, now is probably the time. She was in no hurry to leave. However, recruiters have been reaching out to her on LinkedIn and one company in particular was on her radar.

Sam had done a lot for her company. She set up the Engineering Standards Library in a way that all codified solutions could be accessed by other engineers. As she rose through the ranks, Sam was able to organize information and solutions in a way that improved efficiency, decision-making and profitability for her company.

All that was in the past now as of 3:00 pm this afternoon. She has been inspired to make a new plan and get her future goals in order. Sam calls Christine's husband, Ken, they used to work together at another company and have stayed in touch in a quasi-coaching, mentoring relationship.

Hi Ken, I appreciate you taking the time to talk to me today.

Always Sam, what can I help you with?

My current role just isn't the same, so I decided to respond to one of the recruiters that have been reaching out. I've got a meeting with a potential employer next week and I'm trying to get prepared. My main concern is that I have not been in the game for a while and I've never been good at answering strange interview questions.

You know, after the reduction in force, I was also let go from our former employer. Funny you should ask, because my partner Christine has been helping me with this very topic. She's come up with a cheat sheet for me that I think will help you. Why don't I send it over and you can read through it to see if it works for you? Take a look at the questions, then pick the answers you feel most comfortable going with and expand on it naturally with a story that will engage the interviewer. Feel free to call me with any questions.

Thank you Ken, I'll have a look.

Just keep in mind, your main objective of the interview is a fact-finding mission. Sure, you can glean what you want from their website, the job description, and the 10-K if they are publicly traded. However, you need to find out WHY this role is important to their company and HOW they plan to measure success.

Your main objective of the interview is a fact-finding mission...you need to find out WHY this role is important to their company, what problems they want the candidate to solve and HOW they plan to measure success.

I do appreciate your insight, Ken. What about closing the interview? You were always good at making sure our team was on task for getting things done. I never know what I should be doing after the interview.

I get it, Sam. Think of those critical questions you always asked at the end of our meetings to help me stay on task. Here are some of my favorites during the interview process:

- What are the next steps?
- What is the timeframe for the next steps in the process?
- Where are you in the candidate review and hiring process for this role?
- How many candidates are being considered at this stage?
- Is there anything about my background where you still have questions?
- Would you mind if I gave you a follow-up call in a couple weeks to make sure things are still on track?

Sam was extremely appreciative. After glancing over the questions and sample answers, Sam felt like she was ready for the meeting. Sam was happy to see what Ken had sent wasn't scripted and gave her a chance to craft her own answers to make sure she would come across as poised and authentic during the meeting next week.

1. **Tell me about yourself.**
    a. Tell them about your background and how your specific experiences make you a good candidate for the role.
    b. Explain what you understand their needs to be, "I understand you want to…(be a leader in your industry)", then share how their needs match a problem you've solved in the past.

2. **Tell me about a challenging situation in your last job.**
   a. Talk about a real situation and how you overcame it.
   b. Use the SCORE (*Chapter 1*) storytelling technique to make sure the interviewer gets a thorough understanding of your situation and capabilities.
   c. **Don't talk about problems** you had with a client, your boss or peers.

3. **You don't seem to have much experience, tell us why you think you're qualified for the job.**
   a. Thank them for the opportunity to share more.
   b. Resumes only allow for a little of our experience and sometimes don't tell the whole story; let me tell you why I think I'd be a good fit based on your needs we've discussed.
   c. Highlight the skills you DO bring to the role.
   d. Talk about how you have had to learn new skills in EVERY job and that is one of the reasons this opportunity is so exciting for you to help grow in your career.

4. **You don't have many years of experience, why would you be a good fit for this role?**
   a. Talk about how the role fits in with your short or long-term career path.
   b. Discuss the skills you expect to learn while in the role.
   c. Share which skills you have that are transferable where you could hit the ground running.
   d. Provide examples of projects you have worked on where you gained the skills to be a success in this role.

5. **What was your greatest disappointment in life or in your career? Or greatest crisis? What did you do about it? What did you learn from it?**
    a. Gear the response towards work (not personal life). If they ask about life; again, don't talk about crises with a client, your boss or peers. Instead, talk about what you learned and how you apply those lessons learned today.
    b. My greatest professional challenge was (describe the situation, the role you played, the actions you took, the result, and how you learned and grew from the experience).
    c. Share lessons learned: We turned it into an opportunity because we learned a lot from that project. We learned that you should pilot test the actual script, report success, make adjustments, and then try again. Continuous improvement is a valuable skill and one I apply in every role I've taken on.
    d. Share how it's made you a more valuable (Leader/Manager/Supervisor/Team Member).

6. **What are some constructive criticisms you have received?**
    a. I view all feedback as an opportunity to grow.
    b. Detail-oriented: Some people think I am "nitpicky" but when details are overlooked, problems surface.
    c. Over-communicating: I tend to repeat myself to make sure people "get it" and understand what I am trying to say from several different perspectives. I like to use examples and stories that relate to the individuals I am working with

so everyone understands from their own perspective.

d. Passion: I have been criticized for my passion, sometimes others I have worked with don't share the same enthusiasm or vision I have for the role I play in organizations and have even asked why I work so hard.

7. **What are your weaknesses pertaining to this job?**

a. The fact that I have never been a [insert title here] in the [insert Industry here] does not adequately summarize my transferable skills. Someone's perception that I have never done "X" may lead them to think I can't handle the job, but there is nothing further from the truth. In my previous jobs, I ... (describe transferable skills based on employer needs).

b. If "X" was part of my job, I would not be of help right now, but I am a quick learner.

NOTE: Please refer to the Appendix section: *What Is Your Greatest Weakness*, for a complete table of weaknesses and sample responses. Use this resource to craft your own response to this important interview question.

8. **What is your management style?**

a. I am a facilitative leader. I like to involve others in the decision and change process because I have seen that it takes less time for people to accept their new reality. I set aggressive goals, monitor progress, make adjustments along the way, and celebrate success.

b. Delegation: I like to delegate to get work done, and I also like to delegate to help people develop within their roles.

c. Succession Plan: My main job is making sure that the people I work with can take over when I'm out of the office, on vacation, or ready for my next role.

d. I also believe that management is a one-on-one relationship with the people I work with. No one style can effectively move a team forward. You first need to understand each individual's goals, and manage the work in such a way that each person is gaining what they need personally and professionally for success.

e. After explaining your style, ask, "Do you agree that this style would fit with your environment and mission?"

9. **Where do you want to be in 5 to 10 years?**

a. NEVER MENTION TITLES!!!
   - Talk about increased responsibilities
   - Talk about learning and career growth
   - Talk about the value you want to bring to the role/department/company

b. Having been successful here, I can see myself assuming more responsibilities and overseeing a portfolio of projects while mentoring others.

c. After answering, ask: "What is the typical career progression for someone in this role?"

10. **How have you functioned as a better employee?**

a. I have been given challenging assignments and projects.

b. I have been empowered to make and act upon decisions.

c. I have been available for my colleagues/team/leadership.
d. I have been supported by senior management.
e. I have been provided and given candid feedback to help develop and grow.
f. I have developed a mentoring relationship with my peers and colleagues.

11. **Why are you leaving your present position? Why change your career?**
    a. I would like to use my skills in different ways in other industries.
    b. I would like to help apply my skills in other industries.
    c. I like to collaborate with others on solving their problems and blending my prior experiences to help your company.

12. **Are you available for relocation?**
    a. For the right opportunity, I would consider relocation.
    b. Which company location has the greatest growth opportunity for someone in my role?

13. **What salary are you looking for?**
    a. I would like to be fairly compensated for the value that I bring to your organization and this position.
    b. What's the entire benefit package look like? It would help to know how the entire compensation package is structured to help me put everything in perspective.

14. **What was your salary in your last job?**
    a. I would hate to share a number with you for fear that it would pigeon hole me into an area that would not adequately compensate me for

the value of this position. What does the overall benefit package look like?

b. I would be happy to comment if you could provide what you think is the approved range for the position.

- When they share a range, always acknowledge the higher number, and that you want to keep on talking about the position.
- Remember to state that your salary needs are negotiable after you have a better understanding of the other benefits as part of the whole compensation package.

c. If they ask you the salary range on the second or third interview, respond as follows:

- Are you formally offering me the position?
- Could you put this and the full compensation package in writing? I would be happy to get back to you in a couple days after I have had a chance to talk this over with my partner/spouse/significant other, etc.

15. **How would you wash an elephant?**

a. Describe the process. Questions like these are designed to see how good you are at planning, organizing and executing tasks. It's also seeing how creative you are when faced with unique problems, and how well you adapt when faced with a unique situation.

b. What kind of tree would you be?

- Again, answers the, "Why should we hire you?" question.

- Answers the "How well do you plan on the fly?" and "How well do you fit in our environment?" questions.
- Tests how well you think on your feet.

16. **Who was your best boss? Who was your worst boss?**
   a. You need to do two things: First, accentuate the positive. Second, diffuse anything thrown at you that may be negative. Remember not to name any one person in particular, the answer is about lessons you have learned.
      - Let me tell you what I have learned from all my bosses or
      - I learned something valuable from each of my bosses
      - My best/most challenging bosses:
         1. Set goals
         2. Communicated expectations
         3. Built trust
         4. Provided open, honest feedback
         5. Rewarded results

17. **What was your greatest achievement?**
   a. Keep it professional – "Professionally, my greatest achievement was ..."

18. **What is your philosophy on life?**
   a. The interviewer is looking to throw you off. Practice answering strange questions with a friend. The internet has many examples.
   b. The basics of answering questions designed to throw you off:
      i. Buy Time: "That's an interesting question"

    ii.   Think to Yourself: "What skills or behaviors in this job related to this question?"

    iii.   Think out loud: Let the interviewer hear your thought process

    iv.   Ultimate Stall: "Can we get back to this question after a few other questions?"

19. What was the last incident that made you angry?

    a.   "Angry is not an adjective used to describe me."

    b.   "I have a radar (sixth sense, good instincts, etc.) for identifying potential problems and creating a plan to prevent them" (*describe the situation, the role you played, the result, and how you learned and grew from the experience*).

    c.   "I get disappointed when deadlines aren't met and when clients aren't happy. But I always find ways to turn it around" (*be prepared to share a specific example*).

20. How do you manage stress?

    a.   We all handle stress differently, some people like to _____, I like to _____.

- Go for a walk
- Get someone else's perspective
- Work out
- Run
- Go for a bike ride
- Go sailing
- Go roller-blading
- Go paddle-boarding

Ken taps on the recent call list on his phone to call Sam...speakerphone ringing. Sam picks up on the second ring.

Hi Sam, so what did you think of those questions and answers? Do you feel better prepared for your meeting?

Yes, thank you. I'm wondering if you want to join me at a panel discussion Christine has set up. It's with a couple life-long recruiters where we'll be hearing their perspective from being on the other side of the table.

Sounds good, Sam. Christine told me about the panel too. I guess she knows a lot of us probably need the same coaching. How about the three of us get lunch at the hotel before the panel discussion?

It's a date, see you there.

Chapter 8: Recruiters Perspective

A View Through the Talent Acquisition Lens

"You need a collaborative hiring process."

— Steve Jobs, Apple

> **The hiring process in most organizations starts from within. Employees inside of companies are the first people that hear about open job requisitions. Therefore, our greatest opportunity to get hired starts by knowing people that work inside of companies; NOT by blindly uploading resumes.**

Christine walks into the room to address the audience

I know some of you know each other, and after today, you will all have a chance to meet each other, to grow your network and help each other succeed. In order to help us all in our next career chapter, I invited two of my favorite Talent Acquisition colleagues to share their insights and address your questions. What better way to understand how to get hired than to talk to people responsible for hiring? Please welcome Amy and Russell.

Amy and Russell are sitting quietly on stage with their microphones clipped to their jackets

We would like to pick your brains today and help our audience learn from your experiences as Global Talent Acquisition professionals. What is some advice you would like to share with today's modern career manager to help them get noticed and get their foot in the door?

Russell smiling with anticipation

Thank you, Christine; and thank you all for being here. By a show of hands, how many of you know how corporate recruiters are measured?

Not one hand in the audience goes up

It was a bit of a rhetorical question...today's recruiter has many metrics and measures; we are being measured by:

- The short and long-term performance of people we have hired.
- How well we can sell the company to desirable recruits and get them in the door.
- The ability to help the company grow in times of need.

But above all else, we are measured on how well we manage referrals from leaders inside of our company.

> **Recruiters are measured by how well they manage referrals from leaders inside of their company...for you to get noticed, you need to get your resume forwarded to the recruiter from someone inside the company, preferably a manager or leader.**

So what does that mean for you as a job seeker? For me to notice you, you need to get your resume sent to me by someone that already works inside my company, preferably someone in a leadership or managerial position. You can upload your resume to our company, but the Applicant Tracking System is the last place we look after we have reviewed and interviewed all referrals. We even pay employees up to $3,000 for finding us candidates.

Amy sitting upright in her chair nodding at everything Russell is saying and builds upon what Russell already said

I'd like to add a few things to complement what Russell just shared. We are seeing over 1,200 applications through our Applicant Tracking System for every position. The people that stand out for me are the ones that best align with our company's culture.

So in two words, what would you call that Amy?

Social Smarts.

Christine asking a well-placed moderator question

Can you elaborate on that Amy?

Of course! Most resumes have all the technical qualifications we need for the job, so what we as recruiters need to do is identify the candidate that will best become a member of our team.

Most resumes have all the technical qualifications we need for the job, so what we as recruiters need to do is identify the candidate that will best become a member of our team.

Socially Smart candidates have spent time learning about our company, who we are, what we stand for, what we tolerate, and what we find intolerable. In order for us to want to bring you into our organization, we need to know who you are. Before you were a candidate, you were a human first, you have a history, and you have a physical and digital presence. We want to know all about that before you visit us for a sit-down conversation.

Socially Smart candidates have spent time learning about our company, who we are, what we stand for, what we tolerate, and what we find intolerable. In order for us to want to bring you into our organization, we need to know who you are.

I would have to say that EVERY organization has named *Team Player* as a value or attribute they require of people they want to hire. If you can't prove you can fit in and play nice with others, recruiters are happy to find another candidate with all the same technical qualifications AND the Social Smarts their company requires to bring you on board.

Russell, leaning forward, jumps into the conversation

Since we're on the topic, I'd like to expand on Social Smarts for a moment. When I think about Social Smarts, I also picture "cultural agility", and I don't just mean the culture within the corporate location where you are interviewing for a job, I mean that within organizations, many cultures exist within departments, regional and geographic locations. There are different customs, languages spoken, food eaten, and different etiquette regarding when we talk business and when it's appropriate to engage people in non-work conversation.

> **Cultural agility: within organizations, many cultures exist within departments, regional**

> **and geographic locations. There are different customs, languages spoken, food eaten, and different etiquette regarding when we talk business and when it's appropriate to engage people in non-work conversation.**

It can be a real deal-breaker or career-killer if you aren't savvy enough to understand, incorporate and work within multiple cultural contexts and locations.

Amy nodding in agreement offers additional context for the audience.

Along with being culturally adept within our company, we also take into account the candidate's ability to be culturally aware of our clients and the countries where they operate. Our clients require a certain level of savvy, since they operate across many different time zones and celebrate different holidays it is critical we are considerate when scheduling meetings, conference calls and visits.

There is something else our company looks for in a candidate.

We look for candidates that show they have a healthy appetite to help us succeed. We want people that are joining our team to grow in their career while helping our organization and clients become frontrunners in the industry.

We look for candidates that show they have a healthy appetite to help us succeed. We want people that are joining our team to grow in their career while helping our organization and clients become better in our industry and market.

Russell leans forward

I've got another spin on that situation...It's important that you can demonstrate you are hungry to help, but what happens when the company you are interviewing for is hungry to hire you?

Christine looked puzzled.

What do you mean Russell?

Well, during your first interview, you should ALWAYS ask the recruiter to explain the process, find out how many interviews you are going to have, who you are going to interview with and where. What kinds of questions are they asking me? What type of information are they looking for to make a hiring decision?

Let's say you're told that there are five interviews in the process, but during the second interview, you're getting fewer questions asked of you and instead, the company is asking questions about what it would take to get you onboard.

If you sense this starts happening, you have probably impressed someone during the interview process and the recruiter has been given orders to get you on board! If this is the case, you are in the driver's seat and are in a much stronger position to negotiate, because they are hungry to have you join their team.

> **ALWAYS ask the recruiter to explain the process, find out how many interviews you are going to have, who you are going to interview with and where. What kinds of questions are they asking me? What type of information are they looking for to make a hiring decision? If**

> **the process gets shortened, you're probably being sold on the position, which gives you leverage while negotiating the offer.**

Amy chimes in

> Along with getting into the company, it's important to stay with the company and make connections along the way. Having a relationship with the recruiter that helped get you in the door can also help keep you in the door.

> Your recruiter already has a network of people inside the organization that can help you. So along with your team, your recruiter can get you connected in ways your team may have forgotten.

Christine provides some additional anecdotal information

> I've worked with many of you in this room to help you in your career.

Regardless of your career level, you need to be able to make sure your story is heard during the interview.

> Many of you have already developed stories, remember the SCORE model (**Chapter 1**) of story development? Russell and Amy have given us six behaviors employers want when hiring a new team member to join their company's culture. There are 60 more just like this.

Russell comments

Christine is absolutely right. Our corporate website shows exactly what our values and mission are, and all three of those behaviors I mentioned we seek during the interview process.

Amy elaborates

If you're going to work for a publicly traded company, Google their 10-K. The 10-K is an annual report required by the U.S. Securities and Exchange Commission (SEC). The first section of the report will tell you their goals, strategy and objectives, which can give you great insight into the company, its customers and how they expect to succeed in the market.

Russell expands the topic further

Few people know this, but the 10-K is required for all companies with more than $10 million in assets and a class of shares held by more than 2,000 owners whether the company is privately held or publicly traded. Smaller companies use a form 10-KSB. These are free and can also be found in the EDGAR database on the SEC's website.

The more you know about a company before a meeting, the better positioned you will be to align your resume and prepare intelligible questions to show that you have done your homework.

Christine adds to the conversation

Along with key business strategy and financial information, pay attention to the Risk section of the 10-K. Chances are the company has significant concerns and if they can find a candidate that can help mitigate or eliminate a risk on this list, that candidate would be an incredibly valuable asset in the company's success.

This has been incredibly valuable Amy and Russell, what closing thoughts do you have for our audience today?

Amy and Russell smirking and looking at each other. Amy leads the conversation.

For me, the top three pieces of advice I'll share are:

1. **Be Aligned** - Your digital presence and in-person presence needs to be the same, AND need to be aligned with the role you are seeking and the company's culture.
2. **Do Your Homework** - There is nothing worse for a recruiter during the interview process that has to teach the candidate everything about a company when most information is available online.
3. **Customize Every Resume** - Before we start our conversations, if you aren't an internal referral as Russell outlined, first you need to get noticed by our Applicant Tracking System. Make sure the keywords for the position are embedded in your resume, which will help get you noticed.

Russell compliments Amy's list

My top three include:

1. **Quantify Your Contributions** - Most resumes list tasks assigned or completed, but the ones that stand out for hiring managers are the ones that have a dollar or percent to get my attention.
2. **Develop your Stories** - Not all people in the interview process are very savvy. In order for you to get noticed,

you'll need to get your stories across, like the SCORE model mentioned earlier. Stories help interviewers understand that you are capable and confident.

3. **Work your Brand** - When someone Googles you, what are the top results? What will they find? You need a brand that companies want to have on their team. Your digital thumbprint is everywhere, so make sure it's something to be proud of.

Christine closes with this sentiment

Thank you Amy and Russell, it's been a productive panel discussion and you've given our audience some great ideas they can apply immediately. You all have a lot to think about and process after today's session. Please refer back to the chapters in the Modern Career Management book I'm handing out today. I've been working with a number of you on your career transitions and progress, and this book has all the key skills you will use during every transition. I hope this serves as a friendly reminder of how to stay on track to working in the career of your choice.

Chapter 9: Negotiating Job Offers

Negotiating offers will differ slightly depending on your career level. After all, the more capability and experience you have, the more valuable you may be to a potential employer. If you've done your homework and you understand what the job is worth relative to the market, the total compensation package and benefits, then you will know when you're getting a good offer.

Perhaps the salary isn't quite where you want it to be, but your commute is now 10 minutes from home, or maybe you don't need a vehicle to commute, or perhaps you can work from home three days a week. You need to look at the offer as a whole package (not just the salary) before accepting or rejecting an offer. Keep in mind, your salary is only a percentage of the total cost you incur to the employer. Companies today are becoming savvier to calculating your cost and the benefit you bring to the company, and their investments in you.

Make sure you truly understand the other investments a potential employer is using to make an investment in you. If you don't know, ask! Find out what employee programs and benefits they offer that makes them stand apart from their competitors. Salary and benefits make up the whole compensation package. The more you understand what they have to offer, the better you will be in a position to negotiate.

Why wouldn't I just take the offer they give me? If you are going into a senior or managerial or leadership position, you are expected to negotiate. People in these positions are always negotiating for their people, resources, equipment, and projects. If you can't demonstrate that you can stand up for yourself in the hiring process, what kind of leader will you be if you just accept what is handed to you? It could create perceptions of you and have your potential employer questioning whether or not you are strong enough for the role.

They are interested in you and you are interested in joining their team. Negotiating is just a formality, an interim step between them agreeing to hire you and hiring you.

When considering an offer and negotiating, consider this list and help build your case to ask for more, or perhaps keep your mouth shut because the offer is so much more than just a salary:

Benefit	Yes	No	Negotiable?
Retirement Plan [401(k) / 403(b)]			
Retirement Plan - Company Match			
Company Stock Grants			
Employee Stock Purchase Program			
Medical Insurance			
Dental Insurance			
Vision Insurance			
Life Insurance			
Life Insurance for Spouse, Child, or both			
Wellness Program/Gym Reimbursement			

Benefit	Yes	No	Negotiable?
Financial Wellness Incentives			
Professional Development			
Career Path/Internal Opportunities for Advancement			
Improves my Commute			
Work from Home			
Annual/Periodic Bonus			
Paternal Leave			
Employee Merchandise Discounts			
Paid Time Off/Vacation/Company Holidays			
Commuter Perks (Rail, Rideshare, Parking)			
Company-issued Tech (Phone, Laptop, Home Office)			
Job Title			
Relocation Expenses			

Benefit	Yes	No	Negotiable?
Professional Memberships/Trade Associations			
Severance Agreement			
Authority/Decision-Making			
Budget Management			

List whatever benefits are important to you and determine what you MUST have versus what you would like to have. Put an asterisk next to these. Next, notice the "Negotiable" column...Make sure you know going into the negotiation what IS and what IS NOT negotiable. It can be painful and embarrassing if you are pressing the company to change something that is not within their control.

Rules for negotiating

- Smile, stay positive: they made you an offer!
- Be curious, clarify you are talking to the right people, the ones with the authority to help the two of you to come to an agreement.
- Ask questions. Don't make demands, this isn't a hostage negotiation!
- Listen more than you talk - the person that talks too much usually loses the negotiation.
- Make comments about how they win by hiring you.

The three areas of most negotiation include:

1. Salary
2. Signing Bonus
3. Performance Bonus Percentage

Sometimes companies are more flexible on one than the other. After being given information on either salary or signing bonus, learn more. Most companies are trying to stay within a certain range because the budget only allows for so much of each. Ask them:

"Where does this fit into the range?"

Be honest. Let them know you've done your homework. Use resources like Indeed.com, Salary.com, Glassdoor.com and compare what the salary is for the position you are seeking with the offer you have in front of you.

"After our conversation the other day, I thought we were more aligned in what the offer would be. Considering my experience we both agreed that I could have an immediate impact on the team and its outstanding deliverables. I guess I was expecting a different number?"

Be creative. Show you are interested and genuine in your pursuit of striking a deal that works for both of you. Find out what you need to demonstrate to be at the top of the range. Then start finding out even more:

"What is the possibility of getting reviewed after my first 90 days, after I prove my value in that timeframe, would the company be open to review my salary and see what other adjustments could be made?"

Use the same cadence to open a discussion on incentive compensation and bonuses. It is possible the company has a discretionary way to recognize exemplary performance. Remember, just doing your job well isn't enough - that is the minimum expectation of the company hiring you. If you want to be recognized, you're going to have to come to the table with something you will do to have a real and lasting social, procedural or financial impact.

The negotiator makes you an offer:

> **Candidate Response: "Thank you! I'm looking forward to taking this to the next step. Hmmm...it's a good offer...is this the best we can do?"**

> **Negotiator: "What's the matter, you seem disappointed?" or "What's the matter, that's a good offer?"**

> **Candidate Response: "It's a good offer, but I've done my homework and I was expecting it to be closer to $"**

> **Negotiator: "We can't go that high."**

> **Candidate Response: "How high can we go?"**

The negotiator in many instances isn't the hiring manager, but sometimes it is. Make sure you stay professional. There is nothing personal about a negotiation; it's just a business transaction between two professionals.

Be thankful and show humility. Arrogance will not help your cause. Standing your ground is important by respectfully engaging in a dialogue and providing the research you have performed. Knowing what you are worth and what other companies are offering for similar roles is a great tactic.

After the company provides you with something to think about, go think about it. Make sure you take time to review any decision with someone else. If you're married, make sure you involve your partner. Never make a decision on the spot, always take time to reflect.

The Offer

There is an old saying, "Talk is cheap." Make sure the offer is in writing. Make sure the offer includes everything you discussed and agreed you would receive as part of your total compensation package.

Chapter 10: You're Hired! Now What???

According to McKinsey, up to 50% of new leader transitions fail within two years.[9] Why? Because people in more senior positions often don't have a structured orientation or onboarding program. Once you reach a certain level, companies expect you to "get it", and by hiring you, and it's up to you to map out and execute a path to success.

According to DDI's Frontline Leader Project, 57% of employees quit because of their boss[10]. There are two ways to look at this:

1. The boss lacks proper leadership and/or organization skills.
2. The employee lacks the ability to deliver what the boss wants.

You may be lucky and have a plan laid out for you. If you're new to the workforce, this is usually the case. Just like school, your courses are all picked out for you. But if you've had some years in the workforce already, you'll be expected to manage your own success.

One of the critical components of your personal onboarding will be to gain agreement by your manager and internal clients (internal client: anyone who depends on you inside the company as a solution provider or team member). Where does the content come from to build your plan? It comes from all the information you gathered during the interview process. Create a draft; then review it with your manager.

Leverage your manager and his or her contacts within the company to help you get to know all the players, or as we call it in our outline below, "Who's who in the zoo?" The plan below is not set in stone. Your plan will be shaped by what is critical for your new role based on three things:

1. Your observations of reality.

2. What you learn by observing and talking to people in the company and clients of the company.
3. What your manager tells you.

Create an outline using the ***30-60-90 Day Plan*** in the next chapter as a starting point. Fill it in with your "known knowns"; then work with others to add the "unknown knowns" and make your plan a reality. The better you can show your new employer you are part of the culture and understand how to help them, the better chance you have at growing your career.

Remember: the perception of your credibility is a balance between what others perceive as your capability and the relationships you manage with others. You may be VERY capable, but no one likes you because you're not perceived as friendly. You may be GREAT at building relationships, everyone likes you, but no one knows if you're really capable of doing anything. Get it? Good. Let's get you on-boarded now.

Chapter 11: 30-60-90 Day Plan

First 30 Days (Who's who in the zoo?)

1. Networking: Meet with everyone involved in the interview process. Why? Because chances are, you're joining a company where you know very few people. Even if you know people, you probably don't have a strong internal network. Although the organization chart will show neatly printed solos of functions, most organizations get work done through a matrix of connected people across departments and levels.
   a. Find out who the key people are in each department you need to know.
   b. Ask for an introduction
      i. Get walked to their office.
      ii. Have your contact email the key person.
      iii. Have your boss or contact set up a meeting with the key person.

NOTE: There is political risk here. Make sure your boss is leading the effort if they want. You do not want your boss thinking you are trying to undermine their authority.

2. Conduct an Informal Needs Analysis
   a. What is the perception of what needs to be done from each person you meet?
      i. What are the facts behind the perception?
      ii. What are this person's feelings with regard to the situation?
         1. How will working on the priority improve the individual/department/company?
         2. How will avoiding the priority harm the individual/department/company?
3. Clarify How You Will Be Evaluated

a. What's measured is what matters.
    i. What needs to be done immediately?
    ii. What needs to be done in the next 30/60/90 days?
    iii. What needs to be done in 12 months?
b. Don't assume you know - clarify, clarify, clarify...reiterate in your own words what you understand - this is critical to make sure you're both on the same page.
c. What does your boss want and need?
d. What do your department's clients want?
e. What does the company want?

Days 30-60

1. Draft a plan of how you can help based on your prior experience.
    a. Determine how the needs you uncovered during your meetings align with the job responsibilities agreed upon with your boss.
2. Collaborate with your boss to gain approval.
    a. Make your boss look good!
    b. Work with your boss to share what you've uncovered.
    c. Determine who needs to be involved to integrate what you've learned into ongoing priorities (human capital and financial capital).
    d. Determine if the resources exist inside the organization or if you need to request funding to hire outside expertise.
3. Follow-up.
    a. Share what has been approved.
    b. Share when you, your team and/or your boss will expect to get the priority scheduled and completed.
    c. Ask for support and resources if necessary.

Days 60-90

1. Enlist Coaches and Mentors.
   a. After you've successfully completed something, go back to your contacts.
   b. Find a mentor.
      i. Enlist someone to be your coach or mentor.
      ii. Ask your boss who would be a good coach or mentor along with them.
      iii. Ask one of your contacts who would be a coach or mentor.
   c. Determine what situations they are most suited to support you.
2. Learn how things really get done in the company.
3. Gain approval to join a project team or kick off a project (depending on your level).

Days 90-180

1. Follow-up with your boss.
   a. Share what you have learned.
   b. Share what you still would like to learn.
      i. Ask for best ways to learn formally and informally.
   c. Discuss opportunities where you can help and how it aligns with where the organization needs the most help.
   d. Discuss situations you are facing and how you propose overcoming challenges.
      i. Seek out advice from your boss, coaches, and mentors.
2. Develop partners across company departments/business units.
   a. Work with others to determine how you can partner to help the company and each other succeed.
      i. Uncover their goals.

        ii.   Share your goals.

        iii.   Determine where shared goals exist.

3. Understand Office Politics.
   a. Find out how things really get done.
   b. Find out how projects get approved.
   c. Identify and enlist key stakeholders at all levels.

Note: Underlying processes aren't usually outlined or written anywhere, so as a new person in the role you'll want to not only take great notes but build your own process map on how things get done.

Appendix

Action Verb Table

accelerated	conceptualized	extended	mapped	regulated	submitted
accomplished	conducted	facilitated	matched	rehabilitated	substituted
achieved	considered	filed	mediated	related	succeeded
addressed	constructed	filled	mentored	reorganized	suggested
advanced	contracted	financed	met	repaired	summarized
advocated	controlled	focused	mobilized	replaced	superseded
allocated	converted	forecast	modified	replied	supervised
answered	corrected	formed	moved	represented	surpassed
appeared	counseled	formulated	navigated	researched	surveyed
applied	counted	fostered	negotiated	responded	systematized
appointed	created	gathered	observed	restored	tackled
appraised	dealt	generated	operated	retained	taught
approved	decided	granted	ordered	revamped	terminated
arranged	delegated	helped	participated	reviewed	took
assessed	delivered	identified	perceived	revise	toured
assigned	demonstrated	incorporated	performed	scheduled	traced
assumed	described	increased	persuaded	screened	traded
assured	designed	indexed	pioneered	secured	transcribed
authored	determined	influenced	planned	selected	transferred
authorized	devised	initiated	prepared	served	translated
automated	directed	innovated	presented	serviced	transported
awarded	discussed	installed	processed	set up	traveled
bought	distributed	instituted	produced	set	treated
broadened	documented	instructed	prohibited	shaped	trimmed
brought	doubled	insured	projected	shared	tripled
cataloged	drafted	interpreted	promoted	showcased	turned
caused	educated	interviewed	proposed	showed	tutored
centralized	effected	introduced	provided	simplified	umpired
changed	eliminated	invented	publicized	sold	uncovered
clarified	enabled	invested	purchased	solved	understood
classified	endorsed	involved	pursued	sorted	understudied
closed	enforced	issued	quantified	sought	unraveled
co-authored	engineered	joined	questioned	sparked	updated
collaborated	enlarged	kept	raised	spearheaded	used
collected	enlisted	learned	ranked	specified	utilized
combined	ensured	leased	rated	spoke	verbalized
commented	established	lectured	reached	staffed	visited
communicated	estimated	licensed	realized	started	waged
compared	evaluated	listed	received	streamlined	weighed
compiled	executed	lobbied	recommended	strengthened	welcomed
completed	expanded	logged	reconciled	stressed	widened
composed	experienced	made	recorded	stretched	won
computed	explained	maintained	redesigned	structured	worked
conceived	expressed	managed	reduced	studied	wrote

What Is Your Greatest Weakness?

Don't make up an answer. Have a work-related answer prepared. Engage the interviewer in a conversation. Sure, you can break the ice by saying, 'I have a weakness for chocolate', but the person interviewing you wants to know what may be a perceived weakness or a weakness you are working to overcome. An overused strength may sometimes be perceived as a weakness. Think about the questions below to create your own response to this challenging interview question; then have a look at the table and see what else may relate to you.

1. What am I really good at while working?
2. What is a "strength" that could be perceived negatively by others in the office?
3. How can I explain weakness as an overused strength?

Example: Foreign Language

I see that a lot of the company's clients are based in South America. While I've never been fluent in Spanish or Portuguese, I've been using some online tools to learn some phrases to help me get by. How useful would it be for me to become more proficient? What kind of immersion programs does the company recommend to help employees?

My Strength	Negative Perception	Interview Explanation
Networking Up	Brown-noser, suck up	I've been in many situations where my teammates were too shy to approach management. While I take the initiative to get management buy-in, sometimes people look at this as me sucking up to management. So to prevent any hard feelings, I always

My Strength	Negative Perception	Interview Explanation
		introduce my connections to my colleagues.
Networking Across	Job hopper, lack of loyalty, usurping authority, not respecting authority or hierarchy	Since companies today are highly matrixed, I've found to get things done I really need to use my networking skills to connect to other groups and departments that have an interest in our projects. I've done this without my boss's involvement, and it's been perceived as me going over my boss's head or stepping out of rank. So I always make it a point to get permission from my boss or invite my boss to join me when I sense the project needs external department involvement in order to succeed.
Quality Work	Overachiever	I've been accused by my teammates as being an "overachiever" because I demand high quality work. Rather than slow progress and wait for the perfect solution, I've learned to get to 75% satisfied with where I am with something; then I invite others in for feedback to get additional perspective to finalize the deliverable.
Direct Communicator	Curt, Mean, Blunt	I've been in many projects where the team agrees we need direct communication to succeed. Unfortunately, some people have perceived my directness for being insensitive, but I find that being

My Strength	Negative Perception	Interview Explanation
		candid is the best way to make sure the team knows what I'm seeing and what is going on. I've learned that in order to communicate effectively with all audiences I first need to understand what they want to talk about first. Then, depending on how they like to receive information, I present the information in a manner that matches their preference for receiving information. Sometimes it's actually better to ask questions before blurting out information so I better understand what the person I'm talking to needs to hear. For example, my boss just wants bullet points, but my team members want to talk about their weekend or the evening they had out with their friends, or the latest show they are binge watching before we can get down to business.

My Strength	Negative Perception	Interview Explanation
Enthusiastic	Lively, Fake, Cheer person	I've learned that not everyone in a team or on a project has the same level of enthusiasm. I'm passionate about work and I have an expressive personality, but that doesn't always mesh well with everyone. So I do my best to engage with my boss, clients and team members in a manner they prefer. For example, my boss just wants bullet points, but my team members want to talk about their weekend or the evening they had out with their friends, or the latest show they are binge watching before we can get down to business.
Questioning Skills	Doubtful, Naysayer, Interrogator, Critic	Sometimes in a team, people feel that I'm slowing progress down with the questions I'm asking. This is inappropriately perceived as being doubtful or critical. I have a genuine interest in ensuring our success on a project. If I sense the team is adopting a poor perception of my questions, I make sure to clarify that my concern is the success of the project. If our project or deliverable isn't right, we risk implementing a solution that doesn't work or hurts people, the environment, equipment or the company's reputation.

My Strength	Negative Perception	Interview Explanation
Self-Sufficient	Cowboy, Maverick, Selfish, Loner, Disconnected	I'm very self-sufficient. Once I know the scope of my work and the tasks I need to get done, just let me put in my headphones and go! Unfortunately, some team members feel like I'm not interested in being part of the team, but there is nothing further from the truth. So to mitigate this, I make sure I spend time "teaming" with my teammates. Then, when the timing is right, I like going out to lunch or visiting with folks over coffee in the morning to catch up. Otherwise, I could probably lock myself in my office and not see anyone all day, and that can create a negative perception.
Overachiever	Brown nose, Scope Creep, Gold-plater	I've learned that some tasks and projects require us to stay within scope. As an overachiever, it's easy for me to want to gold plate everything instead of delivering the stainless steel solution the project demands. If everything that had to be done on a project had to be done perfectly, projects would quickly run out of time and money. So I'm very careful to stay within scope so we don't go through our budget or resources unnecessarily. In many situations, striving for perfection may not be what the task calls for. I've

My Strength	Negative Perception	Interview Explanation
		learned it's best to do what has been asked of you to make sure the person that assigned me the task is getting what they expect, which is what is most important when working in a team or on a project.
Patient	Not Caring, Smug, Lazy	I'm a very patient person, but sometimes, on a team, that can be perceived as not caring, but I do care, and sometimes caring means you need to give people space to get their work done. On teams, an interesting dynamic emerges: there are always a few people that think they are doing the work and no one else is doing anything. So in order to debunk that myth, I have taken advantage of virtual tools like Microsoft Teams and Trello so everyone can see all of the team's tasks, who is working on what and what is happening next. We discuss our team's responsibilities and progress weekly to prevent any misinformation from being created or spread. Unfortunately, in a team, a lack of information or communication creates a gap, which is usually filled by gossip; and it's up to the leader/manager/supervisor to make sure everyone stays on the same page.

My Strength	Negative Perception	Interview Explanation
Cooperative	Risk Averse, Non-Confrontational	Some team members have viewed my cooperation with others on the team and outside our department as being "conflict averse", but that's not true or healthy for a project or team to progress. When I sense there are differences I don't like letting those play out in a public setting or in a meeting where the agenda doesn't have room for additional content. I prefer to set up time one-on-one with others to clarify their needs. Then, if necessary, I will call a separate meeting for us to have a healthy discussion so we can all get on the same page and keep the project moving forward.
Proud	Hermit, Loner	I used to not like asking for help. I figure, the boss and my team members trust that I can get this work done, so I'm going to do it. However, I've learned that spinning my wheels and not making the progress I want can keep the task from getting completed, which could impact others. So I've learned to ask for help as soon as I run into a situation that warrants. I've learned that my team members, my boss and even my clients are more than willing to give me their knowledge and wisdom – all you need to do is ask.

My Strength	Negative Perception	Interview Explanation
Reactive	Spaz	I like to be very responsive when the situation calls for it. But sometimes, my responsive nature can be misinterpreted. In situations where I get excited to respond, I like to ask more questions before providing a flood of information. This helps me offer the right level of response and support depending on the situation.
Helpful	Know-it-All	I sometimes have a tendency to say "yes" to every opportunity to help folks on my team. But I've learned that isn't always what the team needs or my boss expects. So I've learned to run everything by my boss first to make sure my priorities are in order before volunteering to take time away from what I need to be focused on.
Enjoying the Work Delegating	Lack of Delegation	I really like doing the work that we do, but I realize that there are other people on the team that also like the work. When I first started managing others I continued doing the work, I was a hero manager. But I realized that my team members weren't growing, and it was because I wasn't delegating anything that was interesting or challenging to them; I was keeping all the fun work for me. So I've learned that to be a good leader and to have an effective team,

My Strength	Negative Perception	Interview Explanation
		you need to learn what interests your team members and delegate work that helps them grow and keeps them engaged. Being a leader or manager is about letting go to help others grow.
Sharing Success	Brag, Gloat, Swagger	I've always taken pride in my ability to share my team's success with others. However, not everyone in a department or company wants to hear how you have succeeded and sometimes perceive it as bragging. So when I am asked to publish something on our SharePoint or Intranet site, I'm always careful to cite all of the contributing factors that led to our team's success and how we expect it to help the company move forward. Otherwise, you could end up with some people thinking you are sharing the information solely to promote your own position and interests.
Communicator	Gossiper, #FakeNews	Communication doesn't always happen through formal channels in a team. Most of the time, larger communication and team health can only be managed one-on-one within the team and department and sometimes involving other departments. I wasn't always good at sharing the intent of these visits or the content of the conversation.

My Strength	Negative Perception	Interview Explanation
		Unfortunately, some perceive this behavior as gossip because they see me talking to different people about different things and when they aren't in the conversation, they usually think the worst. In order to manage this perception, I always name who I have spoken with to clarify content and intent, this prevents other gossip from being spread unnecessarily.
Managing	Micro Managing, Nosy	Management is a verb, not a noun. It's our job as managers to make sure we know what needs to get done and we know the people that have been assigned the work are competent. I made a mistake early in my career assuming that people knew what they were doing. I learned quickly that people need the right balance of direction and support to succeed. Rather than question everything of everyone (which is micro managing) I spend time asking questions to gauge people's competence. When I realize they are competent to complete the task, I back off and let the team member know to call when they need help. When I ask a newer team member to describe how they will handle a task and it is clear they will spend more time than necessary, I let them know I

My Strength	Negative Perception	Interview Explanation
		think there is an easier way for them to get the work done; then get their permission to share. Nine times out of 10 the team member is elated that I took the time to coach them. The 10th person, I will let them struggle a little while, then when I check in on them they always ask what I would recommend.
Consensus	Wasting Time, Not Exercising Authority, Playing Politics	In today's highly matrixed organizations, consensus needs to exist before ideas, initiatives, projects, or budgets are approved. Without the proper level of support, a project or initiative is doomed to fail. Some have accused me of spending too much time politicking to get work done, but I've learned the hard way that without consensus, you can't get what you need to succeed. I've learned that in order to gain consensus you need to sell the benefits of change. Most leaders/managers/supervisors tell team members what they want to do without selling them on the benefits of changing. It takes a little more time, but calculating the financial and emotional benefits of change and presenting your case in a logical manner, it's easy to get people on board.

Turning Contributions into Numbers

How would you like to see bullets like this in your resume?

- 10% improvement in satisfaction surveys
- 20% increase in employee retention
- 30% more profitable
- 40% increase in sales
- 50% increase in client retention

Who wouldn't? Numbers show that you understand the Return On Investment (ROI) and impact you have had at work. Can you only show numbers that you personally contributed? Of course not, and it's not realistic. Someone, somewhere is measuring the effectiveness of your job. From the executive sponsor through the project worker, everyone is responsible for ROI. Therefore, knowing your project, team, or department's ROI are critical to get you noticed. Take credit for your hard work and include numbers in your resume.

How have you made an impact as an individual, a member of a team or department? Here are some ideas to get you thinking:

- Increased efficiency
- Increased productivity
- Decreased error rates
- Increased quality
- Improved safety
- Increased cost savings
- Improved loss avoidance
- Avoided unnecessary costs

One company our firm worked with helped redesign their training program to earn accreditation from the Project Management Institute (PMI). Big deal, right? Let's look at it this way...the class our client offered had maybe 400 people attend annually in the United States.

Now that the course is PMI-accredited, anyone with a Project Management Professional certification needs Continuing Education Units (CEU) every year. Now that the course is recognized, it opens up their audience from 400 to over 900,000 members globally!

If you think about the numbers behind your work and start asking others about impact, eventually you'll find what you need to add numbers to your story. How can you calculate the actual numbers? You need to ask. No one is going to hand you a neatly completed worksheet with all you need to know. You're going to need to seek out the pieces of the puzzle and put them together yourself. Keep in mind, this isn't math, there is not always going to be an exact answer. Look at the numbers more of an estimate and you'll be fine.

What gets measured, matters

What reports does your boss look at? What reports are sent to the executive team? What reports go to the management team? What reports do the Board of Directors look at? If you understand what metrics the leaders in the company are looking at, see if you can get copies. Then, compare how the numbers are changing after you, your team or your department have completed an important project or made a change that moved the numbers.

Goals, Goals, Goals

1. What are your industry goals?
2. What are your company's goals within that industry?
3. What are your department's goals within the company?
4. What are your team's goals within the department?
5. What are your goals?

Before you can know your ROI, you first need to understand your Key Performance Indicators (KPI) for success. This will tell you where you are currently on the roadmap to success and you can use these measures as a way to clarify whether or not the measures have been achieved. If you don't achieve the desired measure, keep working until you do!

How can I collect that information?

1. Estimate the impact based on what you know.
   a. What is the average salary of a person at your company?
   b. Divide average salary by 250 (working days in a year).
   c. Multiply the cost of working days by number of people impacted.
   d. Multiple number of people impacted by number of days.
2. How much money does your company make each day it is operating?
   a. How many days did your solution save the company from shutting down operations?
   b. How many days did your company operate last year?
   c. How many days did your company operate after your solution was implemented?
3. Innovation
   a. How did your new process save time?
   b. How much is people's time worth?
   c. How many people were impacted?
   d. For how long will people be impacted by your innovation?
4. Surveys
   a. Conduct a survey before your solution.
   b. Ask survey respondents to estimate how much time they are wasting on "X".
   c. Ask survey respondents to estimate how much "X" is costing the company.
   d. Ask survey respondents to estimate how much the company will save after "X" is fixed.
   e. Conduct a survey after your solution has been implemented.

  f. Ask survey respondents to estimate how much more efficient or effective they are now that "X" is fixed.

5. Technology

  a. Find out what technology is used to measure your company quality.

  b. Find out what technology is used to measure your company productivity.

  c. Gather measures before your solution.

  d. Gather measures after your solution.

Metrics by Functional Department [11]

1. Human Resources
   a. Retention/Turnover Rates
   b. Employee Engagement/Satisfaction
      i. Reduced Absenteeism
   c. Exit Survey Data
   d. Great Place to Work
   e. Training and Development
      i. Succession Readiness
      ii. Competence Management
      iii. Work Results
   f. Succession Readiness
   g. Recruiting
      i. Time to hire
         1. All positions
         2. Key positions
      ii. Retention
      iii. Key position turnover
   h. Claim Management
      i. Reduced workers compensation claims
      ii. Reduced unemployment claims
      iii. Reduced harassment claims
2. Operations/Safety
   a. Reduced cycle time
   b. Increased quality
   c. Reduced injuries
   d. Reduced loss time due to injury or incident
   e. Reduced workers compensation claims
   f. OSHA Findings
   g. Employee Claims
   h. Client Claims
3. Sales (Beyond just sales)
   a. Client acquisition costs
   b. Client retention
   c. Client referrals

      d.   Client turnover rates
      e.   Net profit
      f.   Average sale
      g.   Time to close sales
      h.   Funnel management
      i.   Number of new service agreements
      j.   Client satisfaction survey results

4. Finance
   a. Cash flow
   b. Working capital
   c. Debt to Equity ratio
   d. Accounts Payable
   e. Accounts Receivable
   f. Return on Equity
   g. Customer Satisfaction (internal and external)

5. Information Technology
   a. Up time
   b. Network performance
   c. Number of tickets closed
   d. Server availability
   e. Number of issues escalated
   f. Number of issues resolved without escalation

6. Customer Service
   a. Average talk time
   b. Cost per minute talk time
   c. Abandon rates
   d. Average time to resolve client issue
   e. Number of complaints
   f. Number of calls transferred

7. Marketing
   a. Brand awareness
   b. Brand loyalty
   c. Leads generated
   d. Internet leads generated
   e. Cost of lead generation

Metrics by Industry [12]

1. Retail
   a. Average inventory
   b. Gross profit
   c. Net profit
   d. Number of stores
   e. Cost of goods sold
   f. Sales per period (Week, Month, Quarter, Year)
   g. Compared to competitors
2. Manufacturing
   a. Cost avoidance
   b. Cost savings
   c. Capacity
   d. Cycle time
   e. Client complaints
   f. Product defect rate
   g. Percentage
      i. Increase in productivity
      ii. Increase in revenue
      iii. Reduction in defects
      iv. Savings in costs
3. Construction
   a. Number of accidents
   b. Change orders
   c. Downtime
   d. Productivity
   e. Profitability
   f. Quality issues
4. Health Care and Social Services
   a. In-patient admissions
   b. Average length of stay
   c. In-patient discharges
   d. Errors related to procedure or treatment
   e. FTE per occupied beds

Author Biographies

Jim and Brant have been providing career coaching and counseling to friends and colleagues for several years. When the two got together to compare notes, they decided to combine their tips and tricks into an easy-to-read playbook: Modern Career Management.

Jim Molloy is most passionate about helping others succeed. He has over 30 years of work experience. Jim has had over a dozen roles along his career path (after college). His career has taken him around the world and his work has been translated into several languages. Jim has held several senior-level roles in many industries. He has written about, facilitated and lectured government agencies and both private and publicly traded companies on numerous business and professional skill topics. Jim is a member of the Adjunct Teaching Faculty at The University of Houston and previously taught Career Search Strategies in Business (BMGT 367) at the University of Maryland: a required course for all business students. He holds a Master's degree in Training and Organizational Development from Lesley University and earned his B.A. from Stonehill College.

M. Brant Butler focuses his expertise on creating a company culture that fosters safety success through positive behaviors and efficient communication. He has over 20 years of experience in Health, Safety, Environmental (HSE), Leadership Management and Behavior Based Safety. Brant has also held numerous roles along his career, even living in West Africa for 2 years where he ran a technical training center and in his present role was recently promoted to Vice President. Brant actively blogs about safety and has published several stories to accompany his life experiences. Along with holding several environmental and safety-related certifications, Brant attended Lubbock Christian University; he has an MBA in Organizational Leadership and his B.S. in Environmental Management from Columbia Southern University. Brant currently lives in Katy, Texas with his wife and 4 kids.

Contact the Authors

After reading the book, **post a question on LinkedIn** if you have a specific question you would like answered.
https://www.linkedin.com/company/consulting-helps/

Remember to **"follow" us** to see other questions and thread responses to critical career questions.

Contact us if you would like to have Jim and Brant join a conference, meeting or classroom as guest speakers. We are available for one-on-one coaching and instruction. Visit our web site to learn more at:
www.ConsultingHELPSYou.com

Email us at JimandBrant@ConsultingHELPSYou.com

Join our mailing list to receive email alerts when downloadable content, templates and new books become available.

End Notes

[1] Number of Jobs Held in a Lifetime
https://www.bls.gov/nls/questions-and-answers.htm#anch41

[2] How Recruiters Effectively Use Social Media
https://therecruiternetwork.com/blog/how-recruiters-effectively-use-social-media/

[3] How to get a job often comes down to one elite personal asset, and many people still don't realize it
https://www.cnbc.com/2019/12/27/how-to-get-a-job-often-comes-down-to-one-elite-personal-asset.html

[4] Over Eighty Percent of Full-time Workers are Actively Seeking or Passively Open to New Job Opportunities https://www.prnewswire.com/news-releases/over-eighty-percent-of-full-time-workers-are-actively-seeking-or-passively-open-to-new-job-opportunities-300682881.html

[5] Deloitte Finds Millennials Confidence in Business Takes a Sharp Turn
https://en.prnasia.com/releases/apac/deloitte-finds-millennials-confidence-in-business-takes-a-sharp-turn-they-feel-unprepared-for-industry-4-0-210863.shtml

[6] Passive Job Seekers
https://www.prnewswire.com/news-releases/over-eighty-percent-of-full-time-workers-are-actively-seeking-or-passively-open-to-new-job-opportunities-300682881.html

[7] Gen X'ers Overlooked for Job Promotions
https://www.aarp.org/work/working-at-50-plus/info-2019/gen-x-missing-job-promotions.html

[8] A Powerful Resume Lesson From History
https://www.forbes.com/sites/dawngraham/2018/12/11/a-powerful-resume-lesson-from-history/#3d1e6ec71035

[9] Successfully transitioning to new leadership roles
https://www.mckinsey.com/~/media/McKinsey/Business%20Functions/Organization/Our%20Insights/Successfully%20transitioning%20to%20new%20leadership%20roles/Successfully-transitioning-to-new-leadership-roles-web-final.pdf

[10] DDI Research: 57% of Employees Quit Because of Their Boss
https://www.prnewswire.com/news-releases/new-ddi-research-57-percent-of-employees-quit-because-of-their-boss-300971506.html

[11] KPI Examples https://kpidashboards.com/kpi/

[12] KPI Examples https://kpidashboards.com/kpi/

www.ingramcontent.com/pod-product-compliance
Lightning Source LLC
Chambersburg PA
CBHW051732040426
42447CB00008B/1097